first
Fish
·
first
People

Sherman Alexie

Jeannette C. Armstrong

Gloria Bird

Mieko Chikappu

Nora Marks Dauenhauer

Nadyezhda Duvan
with Jan Van Ysslestyne

Shigeru Kayano

Shiro Kayano

Lee Maracle

Ito Oda
with Tomo Matsui

Sandra Osawa

Vladimir M. Sangi

Elizabeth Woody

first
fish

◆ Salmon Tales of the North Pacific Rim ◆

first
People

Edited by Judith Roche
and Meg McHutchison

ONE REEL

UNIVERSITY OF WASHINGTON PRESS
Seattle/London

Published simultaneously in the United States by
University of Washington Press, P.O. Box 50096,
Seattle, WA 98145–5096 and in Canada by UBC
Press, University of British Columbia, 6344 Memo-
rial Road, Vancouver, British Columbia, V6T 1Z2.

Designed by Susan E. Kelly
Produced by Marquand Books, Inc., Seattle
The text of this book is composed in Weiss
and Braganza.
Printed in Hong Kong
First edition

Library of Congress Cataloging-in-Publication Data
First fish, first people : salmon tales of the North
    Pacific rim / edited by Judith Roche and Meg
        McHutchison.
            p.   cm.
        ISBN 0-295-97739-6 (alk. paper)
        1. Indians of North America—Northwest Coast
of North America—Folklore. 2. Salmon—Folk-
lore. 3. Indians of North America—Fishing—
Northwest Coast of North America. 4. Salmon—
Literary collections. 5. Ainu—Folklore. 6. Nanai
(Asian people)—Folklore. I. Roche, Judith.
II. McHutchison, Meg.
E78.N78F47   1998
398.2'08997—dc21   98-18055

Canadian Cataloguing in Publication Data
Main entry under title
First fish, first people

    ISBN 0-7748-0686-9
    1. Pacific salmon—Literary collections.
2. Pacific salmon—Folklore. I. Roche, Judith.
II. McHutchison, Meg.
E78.N78F52   1998   808.8'0362756   C98-910404-4

Contents

Illustrations

Acknowledgments

One Reel project staff:

Louise DiLenge, Project Producer

Judith Roche and **Meg McHutchison**, Editors

Jane Corddry Langill, Project Director

Rie Taki, Japan Projects Manager

Vicky Lee, Project Development

Danielle Bennett, Editorial Assistant

This project was made possible by the generous support of the McGregor Family Fund, the Japan-U.S. Partnership for the Performing Arts program of The Japan Foundation and The Norcliffe Foundation.

Special thanks to:

Sherman Alexie for inspirational input and guidance in the invitation of other participating Native American and First Nation Canadian writers.

Shigeru and Shiro Kayano for tireless research, access to the family collection of Ainu artifacts and archives and recommendations for other Ainu participants.

Furusato Caravan of Tokyo for continuing Japan projects collaboration with One Reel and their gracious efforts on behalf of this book.

Dr. Jane Goodall, whose Roots and Shoots program for children sent us out into the ocean of salmon.

Contributors, advisors, and kind supporters include:

Diane Abt, Rebecca Andrews, Michael Campbell, Karen DeSeve, Mieko Doi, Fumiko Endo, Natalie Fobes, David George Gordan, Vi Hilbert, Junko Hiratsuka, Katsuhiko Ishizuka, Sergei Kan, Norm Langill, Spike Mafford, Katsuhiko Masuda, Susan Matsui, Mitsuo Nabekura, Masafumi Nagao, Hisao Oda, Tomoko Oda, Catherine Person, Deborah Butterworth Robinson, Wataru Sato, Bob Seidel, Takashi Shinohara, Rick Simonson, Galena Volchik, Gary Wingert, Hideki Yoneda, and Michael Zielenziger.

Permissions

Preface

Little more than a century ago, wild salmon made their way up rivers and past waterfalls in the Pacific Northwest to support life and culture on the coast and hundreds of miles inland. Today, the once seemingly inexhaustible fish runs are being declared endangered, and our human solutions to save the soul and symbol of the region—barging, hatcheries, fish farming—are being called into question. It is against this background that I share the short tale of how One Reel came to make this book.

Several years ago, One Reel, a nonprofit producer of arts, festivals and special events, was privileged to work with Dr. Jane Goodall. She encouraged us to use our international friendships and resources in the arts to link children and save the planet. A tall order, but we accepted the challenge and focused on salmon. Why salmon? We had often used the fish as an emblem of the region in joyous local celebrations, but most of all, here in the Northwest, we are haunted by the ghosts of salmon.

We began by talking to our friends in the region and around the Pacific, and the result amazed us. It seemed everyone we knew was no more than one person away from a direct connection to salmon culture: writers, fishermen, tribal leaders, biologists, educators, photographers, environmentalists, politicians and poets. It was as if we had asked if they had any connection to water, or to love. Their knowledge and encouragement spawned our "Wild Salmon Project," which has grown to include international education exchanges and the goal of a theatrical performance tour. *First Fish • First People* is the first step in that multi-year project, as we try to understand the salmon culture of which we are the inheritors and stewards.

This collection of tales, essays and verse grew from a conversational dream woven over a meal shared by Louise DiLenge and Sherman Alexie. Sherman went off to write salmon poems, and Louise and I put our heads together to find a form for the dream. With the assistance of Furusato Caravan Theatre in Tokyo, we contacted Ainu leader, Shigeru Kayano. He led us to other Ainu writers, who led us to a Nyvkh colleague in Sakhalin. On this side of the Pacific, Sherman suggested a number of Native writers, and Judith Roche found others through her literary connections. The trail to Siberia, through snow, slow mail and scarce telephones, was the most arduous but led to rich rewards.

As this book comes to fruition, we embark on the next phase of the project, linking children and elders in salmon communities around the Pacific Rim. We are both encouraged and discouraged about the future of the first fish. We hope that our children will work together to ensure that salmon—not their ghosts—will continue to swim up rivers for future generations to see.

Jane Corddry Langill
One Reel, Seattle

FIRST FISH • FIRST PEOPLE
Salmon Tales of the North Pacific Rim

According to Makah legend, salmon were people before they were transformed into fish and, as fish, they look forward to fulfilling their duty as food for earth people, part of the sacred cycle of life. To the Okanagan people, salmon are the outward expression of God. The Tlingit name their clans and design their crests around varieties of fish. The Ainu of northern Japan call salmon "the fish of the gods."

To all people who come in contact with them, salmon inspire awe and wonder. Born in rivers, they journey downstream to the ocean, travel thousands of miles over several years as they grow and then return to the rivers in abundant numbers, thrashing their way upstream to spawn and die. Today, wild salmon are disappearing rapidly, their homegrounds destroyed by industrial development, greed, dams and the pressure of ever-growing human populations. All around the North Pacific, governments, scientists, environmentalists and commercial interests are spending billions of dollars and millions of words trying to save the fish.

First Fish • First People presents the voices of contemporary writers and storytellers whose traditional cultures flourished on the shores and river banks around the North Pacific Rim where salmon have been coming home to spawn for millions of years. The contributors represent many indigenous peoples: Spokane, Coeur d'Alene, Warm Springs, Colville, Makah, Coastal Salish, Okanagan and Tlingit of North America, as well as Ainu of northern Japan, Nyvkh of Sakhalin and Ulchi of the Amur River in Siberia. Speaking a variety of languages, living in communities separated by thousands of miles, these cultures shared a dependence on salmon for survival and a profound relationship with the cycles of the natural world. All celebrated the sacred fish, many with "First Fish" ceremonies to welcome the salmon home each year and give thanks for the life they provided.

For this book, we asked the contemporary First People to speak about the First Fish. It is intended not as a scholarly review of the subject or a comprehensive survey of Native literature, but rather as an informative and personal inquiry by literary artists. In memoirs, poems, folktales, stories, ancient chants and modern essays, they bring to life a world centered on salmon. Invited to participate for their skill in storytelling, these writers also bring to their work a deep understanding of history and a passionate knowledge of contemporary culture. In contrast to the past, these are not happy times for the Pacific salmon, and through these tales runs a common thread of grief shared by people deeply connected to the noble fish and their historic homegrounds. So much has been lost, even within the lifetimes of the storytellers. However, against this sense of loss and the cacophony of arguments, these modern voices also form a strong chorus of commitment to tomorrow based on a memory of yesterday. So many of these writers also use their skills as teachers, activists and political leaders to bring the beauty and wisdom of their traditions into the future. Central to those traditions is respect for the sacred fish.

Working on this book, we have learned much about respect for salmon, for people and for homelands. We hope that you enjoy your literary journey around the North Pacific Rim with *First Fish • First People.* May the spirit of the wild salmon stay with you and carry you home.

Judith Roche
Meg McHutchison

As we honor the Spirit of the Salmon,
the First People give thanks to
the Creator for informing us that
"The Earth is our first teacher!"
May humans learn to study and listen
to our first teacher so we may all survive
and together honor Earth's gifts.

Traditionally
Vi [taqʷšəblu] Hilbert

Sherman Alexie at the
Spokane River, which flows
into the Columbia and travels
over a dozen dams before
reaching the Pacific Ocean.

SHERMAN ALEXIE

The Powwow at the End of the World

I am told by many of you that I must forgive and so I shall
after an Indian woman puts her shoulder to the Grand Coulee Dam
and topples it. I am told by many of you that I must forgive
and so I shall after the floodwaters burst each successive dam
downriver from the Grand Coulee. I am told by many of you
that I must forgive and so I shall after the floodwaters find
their way to the mouth of the Columbia River as it enters the Pacific
and causes all of it to rise. I am told by many of you that I must forgive
and so I shall after the first drop of floodwater is swallowed by that salmon
waiting in the Pacific. I am told by many of you that I must forgive and so I shall
after that salmon swims upstream, through the mouth of the Columbia
and then past the flooded cities, broken dams and abandoned reactors
of Hanford. I am told by many of you that I must forgive and so I shall
after that salmon swims through the mouth of the Spokane River
as it meets the Columbia, then upstream, until it arrives
in the shallows of a secret bay on the reservation where I wait alone.
I am told by many of you that I must forgive and so I shall after
that salmon leaps into the night air above the water, throws
a lightning bolt at the brush near my feet, and starts the fire
which will lead all of the lost Indians home. I am told
by many of you that I must forgive and so I shall
after we Indians have gathered around the fire with that salmon
who has three stories it must tell before sunrise: one story will teach us
how to pray; another story will make us laugh for hours;
the third story will give us reason to dance. I am told by many
of you that I must forgive and so I shall when I am dancing
with my tribe during the powwow at the end of the world.

That Place Where Ghosts of Salmon Jump

Coyote was alone and angry because he could not find love.
Coyote was alone and angry because he demanded a wife

from the Spokane, the Coeur d'Alene, the Palouse, all those tribes
camped on the edge of the Spokane River, and received only laughter.

So Coyote rose up with his powerful and senseless magic
and smashed a paw across the water, which broke the river bottom

in two, which created rain that lasted for forty days and nights,
which created Spokane Falls, that place where salmon travelled

more suddenly than Coyote imagined, that place where salmon swam
larger than any white man dreamed. Coyote, I know you broke

the river because of love, and pretended it was all done by your design.
Coyote, you're a liar and I don't trust you. I never have

but I do trust all the stories the grandmothers told me.
They said the Falls were built because of your unrequited love

and I can understand that rage, Coyote. We can all understand
but look at the Falls now and tell me what you see. Look

at the Falls now, if you can see beyond all of the concrete
the white man has built here. Look at all of this

and tell me that concrete ever equals love. Coyote,
these white men sometimes forget to love their own mothers

so how could they love this river which gave birth
to a thousand lifetimes of salmon? How could they love

these Falls, which have fallen farther, which sit dry
and quiet as a graveyard now? These Falls are that place

where ghosts of salmon jump, where ghosts of women mourn
their children who will never find their way back home,

where I stand now and search for any kind of love,
where I sing softly, under my breath, alone and angry.

Spokane Falls in
downtown Spokane.

Sherman Alexie

SHERMAN ALEXIE (Spokane/
Coeur d'Alene) was born in 1966 in
Spokane, Washington. He grew up in
Wellpinit, on the reservation outside
Spokane. He attended Gonzaga University, a small Catholic college in Spokane, for two years, then transferred to
Washington State University in 1988.
There he met Alex Kuo, a poet and fac-
ulty member teaching creative writing,
who encouraged him to develop his
writing talent. He published over 200
poems in his years at WSU, but never
graduated.

Alexie worked for People to People,
a non-profit organization in Spokane,
for nine months as program information
coordinator—the only "real job" in his
life. In 1992, he received a National
Endowment for the Arts fellowship and,
after that, book contracts. Many other
awards followed in a very short time, including the Lila Wallace–Reader's Digest
Writers' Award, the American Book
Award, and *Granta Magazine* named him
one of Granta's Best of the Young
American Novelists. He has published
ten books of poetry, essays, short stories
and novels including *The Lone Ranger and
Tonto Fistfight in Heaven*, *Reservation Blues*
and *Indian Killer*.

His most recent venture, the film
Smoke Signals, was the winner of the 1997
Audience Award and the Filmmakers'

Sherman Alexie
performing
Lester FallsApart
at Bumbershoot,
The Seattle Arts
Festival, 1994.

Award at the Sundance Film Festival. It
is the first feature-length film to be both
written and directed by Native Americans with all the Indian roles played by
Native American actors. He is currently
at work on three more films as well as a
new book, *The Sin Eaters*.

SHIGERU KAYANO

Traditional Ainu Life: Living Off the Interest

Translated by
Jane Corddry Langill
with Rie Taki

To the kind readers of this book, Shigeru Kayano sends warmest greetings from the large island at the north of Japan known in the Japanese language as Hokkaido and known in the language of Ainu people who have lived here for centuries as *Ainu Moshir,* "the peaceful land of the people."

In the Ainu language, the word *ainu* means "human," and it could only be applied to a respectable human being, so the word *ainu* was very important in our society.

But after the Japanese began their colonial invasion of Hokkaido, our *Ainu Moshir,* the once-proud designation *ainu* came to be seen as discriminatory. We ourselves did not like to be called *"ainu,"* and even the Japanese were reluctant to say the word.

This was quite unfortunate, but today we are gradually coming to understand the true meaning of Ainu, and the situation is slowly improving.

The Ainu word for salmon is *shipe.* It comes from *shi-e-pe,* which means "the real thing we eat"—our staple food. As the name suggests, salmon was the principal part of the Ainu diet, and it was caught and eaten with care. In particular, when we caught salmon before they spawned we took only the amount needed to eat that day. One reason is that before they have laid their eggs salmon are very fatty, so if split and dried they turn brown with the fat and taste bad, no matter how they are prepared. Knowing this well, the Ainu never caught salmon before they had spawned if they intended to preserve the fish.

This practice was based on long experience and cooperation with nature, and in the years when the Ainu managed the rivers and the fish, they ate only the "interest" on the returning fish, so there was never a worry about the "capital" or main stock of fish disappearing.

But then, from the mainland of Japan to the west, the people we called the *Wajin* moved in like a landslide, without offering so much as a word of greeting to the Ainu people.

The Japanese who immigrated into our land in overwhelming numbers unilaterally

23

An elder (*fuchi*), with tattooed mouth, weaving baskets at her loom.

imposed a ban on the harvest of salmon, an act of Ainu-killing foolishness that robbed our people of the right to a living, and thereby the right to life.

Forbidden to catch their staple food, the Ainu fell into indescribable hardship, with many starving to death. This accelerated the precipitous decline in population.

When I was a child, our fathers secretly caught salmon in the dead of night, cooked it right away and fed it to the children. We were warned that if a stranger ever asked us if we ate salmon, we must not admit it. In other words, to children of my generation, salmon was a food to be eaten in secret.

For human beings, the right to live is closely akin to the right to eat, so whoever you may be, you do not have the right to deprive others of their staple food.

Nevertheless, the Japanese invaded the land of the Ainu, calmly took from the indigenous Ainu their main food, and even made catching salmon a crime—poaching—subject to arrest. Similarly, taking a single tree from our forest was also made into a crime— timber theft—also grounds for arrest.

I would like to tell a personal story which took place long ago, around 1932. One day, the old wooden door to my house was rattled open. A policeman stepped inside, looked at my father and said, "Shall we go, Seitaro?"

My father prostrated himself on the floor and said, "Yes, I'm coming." Without raising his head, he let large tears fall onto the wooden floorboards.

I witnessed this as a very young child, not yet a schoolboy. My first reaction was "An adult is crying!" My next thought was "Tears are falling where I can't see his eyes!" But most upsetting to me was what happened next.

My father was being taken away by the police for catching salmon, the fish that he caught for us and told us to eat without ever telling anyone, the fish you weren't allowed to catch. As my father was led away, I ran after him, sobbing. I remember this as clearly as if it were yesterday, and the memory always brings tears to my eyes.

More than seventy years have passed

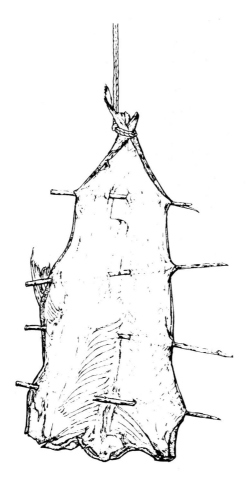

Atat: Salmon that have already spawned are split and dried to eat during winter months.

since my father was led off, but today, Ainu rights to salmon are not yet recognized, and if we attempt to catch a single fish without permission, we can be arrested.

According to the December 1995 issue of the *Hokkaido News*, approximately fifty-two million salmon were caught off the shores of Hokkaido that year, and the November 1997 issue of the same paper reported the annual harvest at forty-seven million.

Of all these millions of salmon, the number legally allowed to the Ainu community living in Noboribetsu was *five* fish, and, until a few years ago, the number legally caught by all the Ainu in Sapporo was just *twenty* fish.

Whenever I talk about the small number of fish that can be legally caught, my acquaintances say, "But Kayano-san, if you would just fill out the application forms, you could get permission to catch fish." But to this I reply: *Ainu should be allowed to catch salmon freely in our homeland without any paperwork!*

From the age of the gods, from the age of the ancestors, the Ainu people have lived on salmon. So I raise my voice to say to the Japanese who invaded our land and stole our fish, "Give us back our staple food!"

I have taken out my passport and traveled to foreign lands some twenty-two times, and I always make a point of meeting with the people who are indigenous inhabitants of the place I am visiting.

I have learned that some kind of treaty was usually made between indigenous peoples and the Europeans who came to colonize, although these treaties were not perfect and were often not honored.

By contrast, there is not even a scrap of a treaty between the nation of

Shigeru Kayano

Japan and the Ainu people. Instead, the "Former Aboriginal Protection Act" was unilaterally imposed in 1899 in the name of protecting the "unenlightened" Ainu.

That law remained a part of the Constitution of Japan for nearly a century, until it was removed just this past July 1, 1997.

At the same time as the "Former Aboriginal Protection Act" was removed, a new law was promulgated with the rather lengthy title of "Law Concerning the Promotion of Ainu Culture and the Dissemination and Preservation of Knowledge Concerning Ainu Traditions."

More popularly known as the "Ainu Culture Promotion Law," this act focuses primarily on the transmission of Ainu language from the remaining speakers to young inheritors of the traditions, and some progress is now being made in this area.

❖

While it goes without saying that language is extremely important in the transmission of culture, I would like to say that Ainu should also be able to catch salmon freely for the sake of transmission of our food culture.

One salmon-catching tool of the Ainu that I believe may be unique in the

Marep: The Ainu salmon spear, featuring a unique revolving hook.

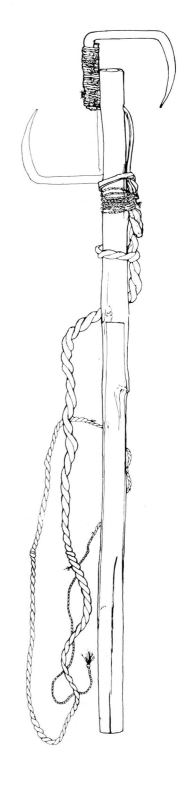

world is the *marep*, a spear with a revolving hook. The *marep* is just one of some fifteen special salmon-catching tools and devices we have developed.

I should also mention that there are at least two dozen traditional ways of preparing salmon to eat, and these traditions must not be lost. Only by going to the river and catching fish with our own hands, using our own tools, can Ainu begin to understand our traditional food culture.

So for this reason as well, I would like the Ainu to gain back the right to catch salmon, the staple food of our culture from the age of gods, the age of ancestors.

I have explained that when catching salmon, we took only enough fatty salmon with eggs to eat that same day. We also harvested, split and dried salmon to help us through the long winter months. For this, we only took fish that had already fulfilled their mission. The leaner flesh of these fish was not quite as tasty, but more than adequate for preservation. In other words, the Ainu took from nature the optimal amount and type of fish to feed themselves without damaging the fish runs. This practice of "living off the interest" of the natural world is an attitude that perhaps we can embrace in our modern society.

The Ainu of old considered nature to be sacred because they saw the sea, the rivers and mountains as divine storehouses of food. If they wanted to eat fish, they ran to the rivers or the sea. If they wanted to eat meat, they went to the mountain forests.

For this reason they celebrated the god of the sea, Atuykorkamuy; the god of the mountain forests, Shirkorkamuy; and the god of river waters, Wakkauskamuy. These gods fed us with food from nature and kept us alive.

No sensible people would destroy or pollute their own food storehouse (nature), and the Ainu people have always been acutely aware of this.

As I write today, in December of 1997, I look at the natural world around me and see dams on the rivers all over Hokkaido, many considered unnecessary by experts, and many with no passage for fish. In so many of the streams of my homeland, not a single salmon can swim upstream.

It is as if we have felled a massive timber across the mouth of each river, a barrier which fish cannot cross. As I am fond of saying, there are hungry creatures waiting upstream—the fox, the crow, the owl, the bear, the *ainu*. For their sake—for our sake—we should move these "timbers" that are blocking the rivers.

Shigeru Kayano

Near his home and museum in Nibutani, Hokkaido, Mr. Kayano recreated this small Ainu settlement *(kotan)* from the turn of the century.

When human beings, myself included, contribute to the ongoing destruction of nature, it reminds me of an old teaching. If we look up into the face of heaven and spit, we can expect it back in our own faces.

Kind readers in foreign lands, I appeal for your support in restoring to my Ainu people the right to catch salmon freely and thereby to preserve our traditions of food culture. I also urge you to come and visit in my home village of Nibutani in Biratori, Hokkaido. As we say in Ainu, *i-yay-rayke-re.* Thank you very much!

(Translated from Japanese.)

Kamuy Yukar: Song of the Wife of Okikurmi

Recited by
Ushimonka Kimura

Transcribed
and annotated by
Shigeru Kayano

Translated by
Jane Corddry Langill
with Rie Taki

The Ainu people living in Northern Japan today are believed to have descended from a large culture which inhabited Hokkaido and the islands to the north as well as some coastal areas of Siberia. Distinct in language and traditions from the ancestors of modern-day Japanese, the Ainu are one of many maritime cultures that flourished and traded all around the rim of the North Pacific Ocean for thousands of years before the arrival of industrial cultures from the south. A lifestyle based on hunting and gathering was maintained in these regions up until the last century.

Blessed with abundance in their surroundings, the Ainu developed a rich material culture as well as a complex array of spiritual practices. The traditional Ainu cosmology ordered all of existence into two categories: human (ainu) or divine (kamuy). Humans interacted every day, in every aspect of their lives, with the kamuy, who were not all-powerful deities who ruled from above, but rather, all the creatures and forces of the natural world. The first salmon who came up the river each year were regarded as the sacred messengers of the kamuy and were treated with respect.

Ainu today are the fortunate inheritors not only of beautiful traditions of weaving, embroidery, wood carving and other arts, but also of a magnificent repertoire of oral literature, including heroic and historical epics, folk tales, cradle songs and long chanted songs about the gods—kamuy yukar. Committed to memory by talented orators, these songs were sung on special occasions. The chanter and audience sat around the fire pit at the center of a traditional Ainu house and a select few kept time by beating on the wooden hearth with a repni (a special carved stick). Although the number of native speakers of the Ainu language is small today, some members of the community can still recite the old tales.

The following kamuy yukar is based on a recitation by Elder Ushimonka Kimura, recorded by Shigeru Kayano in 1961. It comes from the large body of stories about a special kamuy, Okikurmi, who was credited with giving all the arts and practical knowledge to the ainu world, teaching humankind how to build houses, catch fish, hunt and weave. Elder Kimura told Mr. Kayano the background story of this yukar when she recorded it:

"Okikurmi and his wife lived together, up beyond the village of Shikerepe. At one time, famine struck and the ainu of the village were starving, so Okikurmi went out to the oceans and caught many fish and whales. He cooked them all up into a giant pot of stew, and then he sent his wife down to the village,

Shigeru Kayano

to deliver a bowl of stew to each household. She went from house to house, handing a bowl of stew in through the window of each—of course she would never go through the front door. At one house, a man deranged by poverty grew curious about the owner of the beautiful hand that came through his window, so he foolishly grabbed and caressed it. This enraged Okikurmi, who took his wife and stormed back to the land of the gods. Over time, his wife began to miss the human village. Her yearning grew so deep that she fell ill. Deeply troubled by this, Okikurmi tried to help her by creating a vision of the village and the whole Saru River valley, which he painted on the sky. When she saw it, she was restored to health."

The tale is told in the first person, from the point of view of the wife of Okikurmi. Several poetic conventions were followed in kamuy yukar. Repetition of lines and sections was common, as was the use of parallel phrases. Examples of this are pointed out in the notes. A refrain line, called sakehe, is inserted after each line of this poem. We have included the Ainu language transcription to offer the reader a sense of the sound and rhythm of the chant. In recitation, vowels are often doubled for the sake of rhythm, so that a word like chep (fish) may become che-ep.

Mr. Kayano offered us this poem for this volume because of its depiction of a wealth of salmon swimming up the Shishirmuka, the Saru River of his homeland, so many fish that the ones on top burn their backs in the sun and the ones on the bottom scrape their bellies on the pebbles.

—JCL

The hearth (aepoi) was the center of the Ainu home, the gathering place for daily life and special occasions, including chanting of epics.

Kamuy Yukar: My Village Painted on the Face of the Sky

ANNA HO-ORE HORE HORE

For my home village

ANNA HO-ORE HORE HORE

I deeply yearned.

ANNA HO-ORE HORE HORE

Because of this

ANNA HO-ORE HORE HORE

I would not eat.

ANNA HO-ORE HORE HORE

Two meals,

ANNA HO-ORE HORE HORE

Myriad meals

ANNA HO-ORE HORE HORE

Near to my lips

ANNA HO-ORE HORE HORE

I would not bring.

ANNA HO-ORE HORE HORE

And so it was

ANNA HO-ORE HORE HORE

That I became

ANNA HO-ORE HORE HORE

One who was dying,

ANNA HO-ORE HORE HORE

As good as dead.

ANNA HO-ORE HORE HORE

Or so it seemed.

ANNA HO-ORE HORE HORE

And so it was,

ANNA HO-ORE HORE HORE

Alarmed by my sad state,

ANNA HO-ORE HORE HORE

A KOR KOTAN PO [1]

ANNA HO-ORE HORE HORE

ANESHIKARUN [2]

ANNA HO-ORE HORE HORE

TANPE KU-USU

ANNA HO-ORE HORE HORE

TU IPE SOMO A-AKI [3]

ANNA HO-ORE HORE HORE

TUSUI CHE KU-UNI P

ANNA HO-ORE HORE HORE

RESUI CHE KU-UNI P [4]

ANNA HO-ORE HORE HORE

TUKARI KE-EHE [5]

ANNA HO-ORE HORE HORE

A NOTECHIW-UWA [6]

ANNA HO-ORE HORE HORE

AN-AN AYNE

ANNA HO-ORE HORE HORE

TANE ANAKNE

ANNA HO-ORE HORE HORE

RAI KU-UNI P [7]

ANNA HO-ORE HORE HORE

A NE KI HU-U MI

ANNA HO-ORE HORE HORE

UNEKU-UNAT

ANNA HO-ORE HORE HORE

A RAMU KI KOR [8]

ANNA HO-ORE HORE HORE

AN-AN AYNE

1. A (I) KORO (have) KOTAN (village) PO (subject marker)

2. A (I) ESHIKARUN (long for, miss). The speaker is the wife of the god Okikurmi, and she is talking about herself. She is explaining that she was once in a human (*ainu*) village, but now she lives in the land of the gods. Pining for that village, she has stopped eating any food.

3. TU (two) IPE (eat) SOMO (wrong/not)

A (I) KI (do). "Two meals I did not eat."

4. TU . . . RE . . . The use of "Two . . . and three . . ." in parallel lines is a formula often used in Ainu epic poetry. It usually signifies "many" or "myriad."

5. TUKARI (nearby) KEEHE (towards). "Near" here means "close to the food."

6. A (I) NOT (face) ECHIW-U (push) WA (do). Not wanting to eat, she did not bring her face close to the food.

7. RAI (die) KU-UNI P (to be one). "I will probably die."

8. A (I) RAMU (think) KI (do) KOR (while) "While thinking that I would probably die."

Shigeru Kayano

ANNA HO-ORE HORE HORE

That my dear husband

ANNA HO-ORE HORE HORE

Set out one day.

ANNA HO-ORE HORE HORE

The time went by,

ANNA HO-ORE HORE HORE

He was due home,

ANNA HO-ORE HORE HORE

He was past due,

ANNA HO-ORE HORE HORE

And yet he did not come.

ANNA HO-ORE HORE HORE

At long last he returned,

ANNA HO-ORE HORE HORE

And this is what he said.

ANNA HO-ORE HORE HORE

"Oh, beloved wife,

ANNA HO-ORE HORE HORE

For our home village

ANNA HO-ORE HORE HORE

You deeply yearn.

ANNA HO-ORE HORE HORE

Because of this

ANNA HO-ORE HORE HORE

Two meals,

ANNA HO-ORE HORE HORE

Myriad meals

ANNA HO-ORE HORE HORE

You will not touch.

ANNA HO-ORE HORE HORE

If this goes on,

ANNA HO-ORE HORE HORE

And you should die,

ANNA HO-ORE HORE HORE

A KOR YU-UPI [9]

ANNA HO-ORE HORE HORE

SOYENPA-A WA [10]

ANNA HO-ORE HORE HORE

AHUP KU-UNI [11]

ANNA HO-ORE HORE HORE

KASUNO I-ISAM

ANNA HO-ORE HORE HORE

KASUNO I-ISAM

ANNA HO-ORE HORE HORE

KI RUWE NE AYNE

ANNA HO-ORE HORE HORE

AHUP A-AKUSU

ANNA HO-ORE HORE HORE

ENE I-ITAKI

ANNA HO-ORE HORE HORE

A KOR TURE-ESHI [12]

ANNA HO-ORE HORE HORE

A KOR KOTAN-UN PO

ANNA HO-ORE HORE HORE

E ESHIKA-ARUN [13]

ANNA HO-ORE HORE HORE

TANPE KU-USU [14]

ANNA HO-ORE HORE HORE

TUSUI CHE KU-UNI P [15]

ANNA HO-ORE HORE HORE

RESUI CHE KU-UNI P

ANNA HO-ORE HORE HORE

SOMO E E-ENO

ANNA HO-ORE HORE HORE

E AN AY-YNE [16]

ANNA HO-ORE HORE HORE

E RAI WA NE-EWA [17]

9. A (I) KOR (have) YU-UPI (brother). "My brother" here means "my husband." In Ainu epics and sacred songs, the husband is often referred to as "brother." People who do not understand this have mistakenly assumed that incest was common in Ainu culture.

10. SOYENPA (went outdoors) WA (do)

11. AHUP (come inside) KU-UNI (probably did). "KUN" is a common verb modifier placed at the end of a sentence, meaning "probably will," "would," or "so that." In epics, it is frequently lengthened to KU-UNI to fit the syllabic rhythm of the song.

12. A (I) KOR (have) TURE-ESHI (younger sister). "Oh, younger sister of mine" he says, but note that in this epic, this means "Oh, wife of mine."

13. E (You) ESHIKARUN (are longing for). Similar to the first two lines of the song.

14. TANPE (this thing) KU-USU (because of) "And so it was . . ."

15. TUSUI (Two times) CHI (I) E (eat) KU-UNI P (what it is that...). "What you eat two times" or "two meals." The first of another "Two . . . Three . . ." pattern.

16. E (you) AN (are) AYNE (therefore, then). "With you in this condition . . ."

17. E (you) RAI (die) WA (do) NE-EWA (if, in that case). "If you should die . . ."

ANNA HO-ORE HORE HORE
Your death would bode
ANNA HO-ORE HORE HORE
Ill for the land,
ANNA HO-ORE HORE HORE
Ill for the village,
ANNA HO-ORE HORE HORE
And all would suffer.
ANNA HO-ORE HORE HORE
And that is why
ANNA HO-ORE HORE HORE
I went out for awhile.
ANNA HO-ORE HORE HORE
I have painted for you
ANNA HO-ORE HORE HORE
In two scenes,
ANNA HO-ORE HORE HORE
In myriad scenes,
ANNA HO-ORE HORE HORE
Our beloved village.
ANNA HO-ORE HORE HORE
And now I've come back.
ANNA HO-ORE HORE HORE
Quickly, come outside!
ANNA HO-ORE HORE HORE
And see for yourself
ANNA HO-ORE HORE HORE
What I have drawn."
ANNA HO-ORE HORE HORE
That is what
ANNA HO-ORE HORE HORE
My dear husband
ANNA HO-ORE HORE HORE
Said to me.

ANNA HO-ORE HORE HORE
NEWA NE-EYAT
ANNA HO-ORE HORE HORE
MOSHIR E WEN-N PE[18]
ANNA HO-ORE HORE HORE
KOTAN E WEN-N PE
ANNA HO-ORE HORE HORE
NE RUWE-E NE
ANNA HO-ORE HORE HORE
KI WA KU-USU
ANNA HO-ORE HORE HORE
SOYENE A-AN WA
ANNA HO-ORE HORE HORE
A KOR KOTA-AN PO
ANNA HO-ORE HORE HORE
TU NOKA ORO-OKE[19]
ANNA HO-ORE HORE HORE
RE NOKA ORO-OKE
ANNA HO-ORE HORE HORE
A NUYE-E WA[20]
ANNA HO-ORE HORE HORE
AHUNNAN KI-I NA[21]
ANNA HO-ORE HORE HORE
HETAT SOYE-EN PA[22]
ANNA HO-ORE HORE HORE
INKAR KI-I YAN
ANNA HO-ORE HORE HORE
SEKOR OKAI-IPE[23]
ANNA HO-ORE HORE HORE
A KOR YU-UPI
ANNA HO-ORE HORE HORE
ETAYE KA-ANE
ANNA HO-ORE HORE HORE
KIWA KU-USU

18. MOSHIR (the land, the homeland, the country) E (that) WEN (evil) PE (thing). "It would bode ill for the whole land."

19. TU (two) NOKA (forms) ORO-OKE (place). "Two scenes." Another "Two . . . Three . . ." pattern, emphasizing how many different scenes he had painted.

20. A (I) NUYE-E (drawing, describing, painting) WA (did). "I painted scenes of the village."

21. AHUN (to enter) KI-I (did) NA (you know!—emphatic particle)

22. HETAT (Come on, quickly!) SOYE-EN PA (go outside)

23. SEKOR (thus) OKAIPE (the thing there is, the thing we have).

33

Shigeru Kayano

ANNA HO-ORE HORE HORE
But, to go outdoors—
ANNA HO-ORE HORE HORE
Ahh! what an effort!
ANNA HO-ORE HORE HORE
Barely crawling,
ANNA HO-ORE HORE HORE
Dragging myself,
ANNA HO-ORE HORE HORE
I struggled outside.
ANNA HO-ORE HORE HORE
When I looked up,
ANNA HO-ORE HORE HORE
It was just as he said!
ANNA HO-ORE HORE HORE
On the face of the sky,
ANNA HO-ORE HORE HORE
Really and truly,
ANNA HO-ORE HORE HORE
My beloved village,
ANNA HO-ORE HORE HORE
My beloved land.
ANNA HO-ORE HORE HORE
In two scenes,
ANNA HO-ORE HORE HORE
In myriad forms,
ANNA HO-ORE HORE HORE
It was painted there,
ANNA HO-ORE HORE HORE
All around me.
ANNA HO-ORE HORE HORE
And I saw before me
ANNA HO-ORE HORE HORE
The Saru River,

ANNA HO-ORE HORE HORE
SOYENPA-A AN[24]
ANNA HO-ORE HORE HORE
IKI-AN A-AYNE[25]
ANNA HO-ORE HORE HORE
REYE REYE-E AN[26]
ANNA HO-ORE HORE HORE
SHINU SHINU-U AN[27]
ANNA HO-ORE HORE HORE
SOYENPA A-AN WA
ANNA HO-ORE HORE HORE
INKAR AN WA
ANNA HO-ORE HORE HORE
NEWA NECHI-IKI[28]
ANNA HO-ORE HORE HORE
NISHI KOTO-OTTA[29]
ANNA HO-ORE HORE HORE
SONNO PO-OKA[30]
ANNA HO-ORE HORE HORE
A KOR KOTAN-UN
ANNA HO-ORE HORE HORE
A KOR MO-OSHIR
ANNA HO-ORE HORE HORE
TU NOKA O-OROKE[31]
ANNA HO-ORE HORE HORE
RE NOKA O-RO-OKE
ANNA HO-ORE HORE HORE
A NUYE KI-IWA
ANNA HO-ORE HORE HORE
SHIR A-AN KA-ATU[32]
ANNA HO-ORE HORE HORE
ENE OKA-A HI
ANNA HO-ORE HORE HORE
SHISHIRMU-UKA[33]

24. SOYEN (go outside) PA (that) AN (there is). The act of going outside.

25. IKI (do) AN (have) AYNE (then, so) Words of self-encouragement. Not having eaten for days or months, she is very weak, so this is what she gasps as she struggles to drag herself to the door.

26. REYE REYE (to crawl) AN (have done)

27. SHINU SHINU (to creep) AN (have done)

28. NEWA (become) NECHI-IKI (if it should) "As if it were . . ."

29. NISHI (clouds) KOTORO (face) TA (on). KOTORO-TA is elided to KOTO-OTTA. The word KOTORO means face or surface, as in TEKKOTORO (palm of the hand), HURKOTORO (surface of a narrow footpath), etc. This is the expression "painted on the face of the sky."

30. SONNO (real, true) PO-OKA (it was, indeed) "Really and truly."

31. TU . . . Here again we see the formula for emphasizing quantity: "Two . . . Three . . ."

32. SHIR (all around) AN (there was) KA-ATU (forms, conditions). Everywhere I looked, the conditions around me.

33. SHISHIRMUKA was the name of the Saru River in Hidaka County a century ago. Just as the text describes it in the following lines "sparkling and clear, with deer running on the river banks, when I was a child the Saru River was pristine." The Saru River Valley was one of the most important areas for Ainu settlement, and was also known as the home of the god Okikurmi, who gave practical wisdom to human beings.

ANNA HO-ORE HORE HORE

Shishirmuka,

ANNA HO-ORE HORE HORE

Flowing clear and sparkling.

ANNA HO-ORE HORE HORE

In the fields by the banks,

ANNA HO-ORE HORE HORE

Deer running in herds,

ANNA HO-ORE HORE HORE

A herd of large deer,

ANNA HO-ORE HORE HORE

A herd of small deer.

ANNA HO-ORE HORE HORE

So beautifully flowed the river,

ANNA HO-ORE HORE HORE

Shishirmuka,

ANNA HO-ORE HORE HORE

With salmon of small size

ANNA HO-ORE HORE HORE

And salmon of great size

ANNA HO-ORE HORE HORE

Thrashing their way upstream.

ANNA HO-ORE HORE HORE

The sun scorched the backs

ANNA HO-ORE HORE HORE

Of fish at the surface.

ANNA HO-ORE HORE HORE

Pebbles scraped the bellies

ANNA HO-ORE HORE HORE

Of fish on the riverbed.

ANNA HO-ORE HORE HORE

Fishermen tangled hooks

ANNA HO-ORE HORE HORE

Vying to spear the salmon.

ANNA HO-ORE HORE HORE

ANNA HO-ORE HORE HORE

ARPA RU-UKO

ANNA HO-ORE HORE HORE

MATNATA-ARA

ANNA HO-ORE HORE HORE

KENASHI SO KA-ATA [34]

ANNA HO-ORE HORE HORE

NOKAN YUT TO-OPA [35]

ANNA HO-ORE HORE HORE

RUPNE YUT TO-OPA [36]

ANNA HO-ORE HORE HORE

CHI TETTERE KE-E RE

ANNA HO-ORE HORE HORE

SHISHIRMU-UKA

ANNA HO-ORE HORE HORE

PETOTNAI-I TA

ANNA HO-ORE HORE HORE

NOKAN CHE-EP RUP [37]

ANNA HO-ORE HORE HORE

RUPNE CHE-EP RUP

ANNA HO-ORE HORE HORE

CHIHOYUP PA-ARE

ANNA HO-ORE HORE HORE

KANNA CHE-EP RUP [38]

ANNA HO-ORE HORE HORE

SUKUS CHI-RE [39]

ANNA HO-ORE HORE HORE

POKNA CHEP RUP [40]

ANNA HO-ORE HORE HORE

SUMA SHI-IRU [41]

ANNA HO-ORE HORE HORE

CHEP KOYKI KU-UNIP

ANNA HO-ORE HORE HORE

MAREP U KO ETAYE PA [42]

ANNA HO-ORE HORE HORE

---

34. KENASHI (plains, fields) SO (sit) KA (upon, above) TA (on)

35. NOKAN (small) YUT or YUK (deer) TOPA (herd)

36. RUPNE (large) YUT (deer) TOPA (herd). Means a herd of does and bucks.

37. NOKAN (small) CHEP (fish) RUP (school). The generic word for "fish" in Ainu is CHEP, from CHI (we) and EP (eat). The fish referred to here is salmon, which is also called SHI-EPE in Ainu, meaing "the main thing we eat" or staple food. Another polite Ainu expression for salmon is KAMUY CHEP, the "fish of the gods."

38. KANNA (surface) CHEP (fish) RUP (group). This means there were so many fish in the river that the surface of the water churned as the fish were crowded to the top.

39. SUKUS (sunlight) CHI (cook) RE (shines on). There are so many salmon swimming near the surface of the water that the skin on their backs is actually scorched by the sun. A sign of abundance.

40. POKNA (back or bottom) CHEP (fish) RUP (herd) The fish swimming on the bottom of the river.

41. SUMA (stone) SHIRU (scrape)

42. MAREP (spear with hook) U (each other) KO (that) ETAYE (pulling) PA (all). The MAREP is a salmon fishing tool unique to the Ainu, made of a long spear with a special revolving hook on the end. This line describes the scene of fishers tangling up their hooks on spears as they compete for the many fish in the river.

Shigeru Kayano

In the fields by the river banks,
ANNA HO-ORE HORE HORE
Herds of large deer
ANNA HO-ORE HORE HORE
And herds of small deer
ANNA HO-ORE HORE HORE
Raced with one another,
ANNA HO-ORE HORE HORE
And those hunting the deer
ANNA HO-ORE HORE HORE
Chased after them.
ANNA HO-ORE HORE HORE
Those digging lily bulbs
ANNA HO-ORE HORE HORE
Abandoned with scorn
ANNA HO-ORE HORE HORE
Their smaller baskets
ANNA HO-ORE HORE HORE
And scrambled to fill
ANNA HO-ORE HORE HORE
The larger ones.
ANNA HO-ORE HORE HORE
A grove of willow trees
ANNA HO-ORE HORE HORE
Stood forward, on the banks.
ANNA HO-ORE HORE HORE
A grove of alders
ANNA HO-ORE HORE HORE
Stood back, in the foothills.
ANNA HO-ORE HORE HORE
A thicket of reeds
ANNA HO-ORE HORE HORE
Stood forward, on the banks.
ANNA HO-ORE HORE HORE

PET KENASHI KA-ATA
ANNA HO-ORE HORE HORE
RUPNE YUT TO-OPA[43]
ANNA HO-ORE HORE HORE
NOKAN YUT TO-OPA
ANNA HO-ORE HORE HORE
CHI TETTERE KE-E RE
ANNA HO-ORE HORE HORE
YUK KOYKI KU-UNI P
ANNA HO-ORE HORE HORE
ORO CHIPASU-USU
ANNA HO-ORE HORE HORE
TUREP TA KU-UNI P[44]
ANNA HO-ORE HORE HORE
NOKAN SARA-ANIP[45]
ANNA HO-ORE HORE HORE
UKO EMAKPA[46]
ANNA HO-ORE HORE HORE
RUPNE SARA-ANIP
ANNA HO-ORE HORE HORE
UKO ETAI-IPA
ANNA HO-ORE HORE HORE
SUSU NI TA-AYE[47]
ANNA HO-ORE HORE HORE
HO SA HO CHIW-U PA[48]
ANNA HO-ORE HORE HORE
KENE NI TA-AY E[49]
ANNA HO-ORE HORE HORE
HO MAKO CHIW-U PA
ANNA HO-ORE HORE HORE
SUPKI SA-ARI
ANNA HO-ORE HORE HORE
HOSA HOCHIW-U PA
ANNA HO-ORE HORE HORE

43. RUPNE YUT (large deer). This means a herd of mature deer.

44. TUREP (wild lily bulbs) TA (gathering) KUUNIP (the ones who are). The ones who are out busily digging up lily bulbs to eat. Traditionally, women gathered and men hunted. The TUREP, a variety of edible wild lily bulb, was an important food source.

45. NOKAN (small) SARAANIP (bag woven of straw). A soft straw basket.

46. U (one another) KO (that) EMAKPA (to hate or scorn them). This describes the scene of eager gatherers, scorning the small gathering baskets and vying for the larger ones to show others what hard workers they are. Another indication of abundance.

47. SUSU (willow) NI (Tree) TA-AY (grove) E (that one)

48. HO (oneself) SA (the fore) CHIW (come out) PA (all). "In the fore."

49. KENE (alder) NI (tree) TAY (grove). The alder tree is also called KEMNE from KEM (blood) and NE (becomes). Alder bark was said to stimulate blood production, so it was given to new mothers after childbirth, as a tea made by boiling the bark.

A thicket of rushes
ANNA HO-ORE HORE HORE
Stood back, in the fields.
ANNA HO-ORE HORE HORE
I was greatly pleased
ANNA HO-ORE HORE HORE
By what I saw.
ANNA HO-ORE HORE HORE

As soon as I felt better, the
picture vanished from sight.

Her health restored
by the painting on the sky,
the wife of Okikurmi
spoke these words.

(Translated from Ainu and Japanese.)

SHIKI SA-ARI
ANNA HO-ORE HORE HORE
HO MAKO CHIW-U PA
ANNA HO-ORE HORE HORE
ANRAMA-ASU[50]
ANNA HO-ORE HORE HORE
AWE SU-UYE
ANNA HO-ORE HORE HORE

KI RUWE NEAY-YNE
A SHIKETOKO USKOSANU

PROWANO PIRIKANO
ANAN SEKOR
OKIKURMI MATAKI
HAWE AN.

50. A (I, the wife of Okikurmi) E
(that) RAMASU (did like, found
pleasing). "Having seen the condition
of the earthly village where I once
lived, I felt much better."

*The rest of the lines in the song are delivered
in colloquial language, without the refrain.*

37

Saranip: Soft baskets
carried on one's back.
Woven from the bark
of the Japanese linden
tree, in a variety of sizes
and shapes, they were
used to gather food and
transport gear.

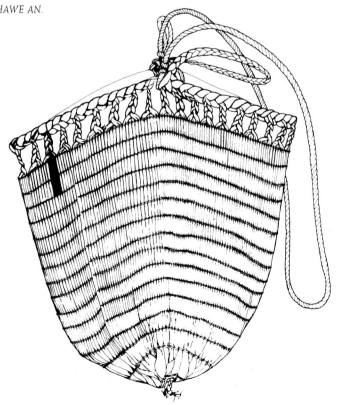

Shigeru Kayano

Ainu men were
expected to master
wood carving *(inuie)*
before marriage.
Mr. Kayano is both
a skilled carver
and a tool and
design expert.

SHIGERU KAYANO (Ainu), born
in Nibutani, Hokkaido in 1926, is a cultural leader in the preservation, study
and promulgation of Ainu language, oral
literature, arts, crafts and ceremonial traditions. As a political leader and member of the Upper House of the Diet, he
led the successful campaign in 1997 for
legal recognition of Ainu as a distinct
people and culture within Japan. Raised
in both Ainu and Japanese, he is among
the youngest of the few Ainu who speak
the language with native fluency. Mr.
Kayano left home at an early age to help
support his family, working in many remote areas of Hokkaido with jobs in forestry, logging, mining and accounting.
He is well known for his definitive
books on tools and crafts, collections
of epic poems and an Ainu-Japanese
dictionary.

In mid-life, he began to devote his
energy to collecting and preserving Ainu
arts, tools and handicrafts of all kinds.
His donation of some 2,000 pieces led
to the founding of the Biratori Township
Ainu Culture Museum in 1972. During
the same years, he also devoted himself
to collecting and translating Ainu stories
and epics. In 1975 he was awarded the
prestigious Kikuchi Kan Prize for his
collection of folktales, *Uepekere Shutaisei,*
and many literary and cultural prizes followed for his large body of work. He

served five terms as a member of the Biratori Township Council and four years in the Upper House of the Diet of Japan. In 1993 he hosted an international forum of indigenous peoples, in connection with the United Nations.

Residing in Nibutani today, he continues his activities as a prolific writer, active leader, chairman of the Ainu language school and director of the museum housing his personal collection of Ainu arts and crafts.

Major publications include: *Uepekere Shutaisei*, 1974, *Kitsune no Charanke*, 1974, *Kaze no Kami to Okikurmi*, 1975, *Okikurmi no Boken*, 1975, *Kibori no Okami*, 1975, *Ore no Nibutani*, 1975, *Honoo no Uma*, 1977, *Ainu no Mingu*, 1978 and 1997, *Chise A Kara*, 1976, *Hitotsubu no Satchiporo*, 1979, *Ainu no Ishibumi*, 1980, 1991 (translated as *Our Land Was a Forest*, 1994), *The Romance of the Bear God*, 1985, *Nibutani ni Ikite*, 1987, *Kamuy Yukar to Mukashibanashi*, 1988, *Tsuma wa Karimono*, 1995 and *Kayano Shigeru no Ainugo Jiten*, 1996.

For further reading and listening:

Kayano, Shigeru. *Our Land Was a Forest, an Ainu Memoir*, translated by Kyoko Selden and Lili Selden (Boulder, Colorado: Westview Press, 1994).

Munro, Neil Gordon. *Ainu Creed and Cult*, edited by B. Z. Seligmann (London: Kegan Paul Japan Library, Vol. 4, 1996).

Philippi, Donald. *Songs of Gods, Songs of Humans: the Epic Tradition of the Ainu* (Tokyo: University of Tokyo Press, 1995).

Watanabe, Hitoshi. *The Ainu Ecosystem* (Seattle: University of Washington Press, 1973).

Kayano, Shigeru. *Yukar: The Ainu Epic Songs*, from the World Music Library (Tokyo: King Record Company, Ltd., 1997).

The inner bark of elm trees (*attus*) is made into a fiber and woven into fabric for robes. Mrs. Reiko Kayano is a master of weaving, embroidery, appliqué and many other traditional "women's arts."

Shigeru Kayano

SHIRO KAYANO

Who Owns the Salmon?

Translated by
Jane Corddry Langill
with Rie Taki

In 1993 the Board of Education of Hokkaido published a book entitled *Trades and Occupations of Hokkaido* and, as a member of the Ainu survey team, I compiled a report on the current state of transmission of traditional Ainu handicrafts. I examined the state of six traditional crafts at that time, among them the making of salmon skin shoes, called *chepkeri* in Ainu. Among the practitioners of this ancient art was my father, Shigeru Kayano. In October of 1992, he made one pair of shoes from the skin of six fish, which had been caught, skinned and dried two weeks earlier.

He chose the skin of the *hotchare,* salmon that have already spawned. The reason was clear: it is thicker and stronger than that of fish who have yet to do so. This selection of the best natural material for making an item for daily use, such as a pair of fish skin shoes, is typical of the large store of practical wisdom accumulated by the Ainu people. In the old days, it was a simple matter to get materials like this by going to spawning grounds and harvesting fish that had already exhausted themselves. Today, however, the Fisheries Agency has given local fishermen's unions jurisdiction over each river and made them responsible for artificial propagation procedures, so the only way to get fish skins now is to go to a hatchery and beg for parent fish that have already been "milked" for their roe or milt.

In our times, salmon is growing ever more remote from Ainu food culture. But in the past, salmon was a major food source. Indeed, in the traditional lifestyle that continued up until 150 years ago, Ainu *kotan* (settlements) were always located along salmon and trout rivers near spawning grounds. Rarely was a hamlet found farther upstream than the fish could reach to spawn. There were certain basic conditions for selection of the place to settle an Ainu village. It had to be a place where it was easy to secure drinking water, where it was easy to secure food, where the ground was high enough to be safe from floods, and where it was reasonably warm, with relatively light snowfalls. The location near salmon grounds was critical to one very important condition—easy access to food. Indeed, the Ainu word for salmon, *chipe,*

comes from *shi-e-pe* and means "the main food that we eat." It was the staple food, the Ainu equivalent of our daily bread.

In the days when the Ainu lived by hunting and gathering, salmon and venison were the main sources of animal protein in the diet. Recent isotope studies of nineteenth-century Ainu bones, hair, blood and nails confirm that the main diet consisted of fish and large marine animals.

Conditions have now changed greatly for the Ainu. The modern development of Hokkaido began with a proclamation in 1876 and the promulgation of the "Hokkaido Salmon Fishing Act" by the government of Japan. By 1878 the Ainu people were forbidden from taking a single salmon from the rivers of their homeland. The one exception was on the upper reaches of the Tokachi River, but in 1883 the Sapporo prefectural government forbade fishing there as well. Within a year of the ban, the Ainu living in that region suffered from severe food shortages and even starvation. Furthermore, in 1896 the "Law of the Rivers" was enacted, putting all rivers under the jurisdiction of the national government of Japan, and many restrictions were included, beginning with the right to fish in rivers.

Even today, in 1998, under the provisions of the "Surface Water Management

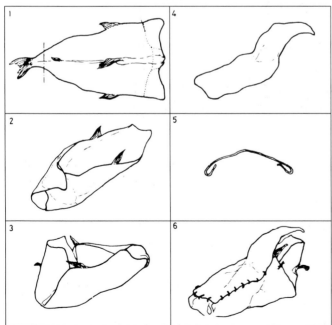

Robe (*attus-amip*) made by Shiro Kayano's mother, Mrs. Reiko Kayano, of *attus* fabric, decorated with appliqué and embroidery designs. Currently on display at the Kayano Shigeru Nibutani Ainu Museum.

(opposite top) Shoes were made of salmon skin by Ainu and many other Northern Pacific inhabitants.

(opposite bottom) Skins were dried, trimmed, folded, perforated with a metal hook and laced together to make the shoes.

Regulations," it is forbidden for an Ainu person or *any* Japanese person to catch salmon swimming upriver to spawn. No matter how many salmon come up the river, catching a single fish is considered poaching and any person caught doing so can be arrested. On the other hand, commercial fishermen with licenses are allowed to catch large quantities of salmon at sea. This harvest is conducted for commercial purposes, not to feed the families of the fishermen.

For the Ainu people, fishing in order to feed our families is completely forbidden on either ocean or rivers. In all of Hokkaido, only a scant few hundred fish may be caught, and only when special permission has been granted by the

Shiro Kayano

The Saru River (*Shishirmuka*) begins in the mountains of Hidaka and runs through Nibutani to the Pacific Ocean. A large dam was recently constructed on the river in Nibutani.

governor. Moreover, these permits are granted for a limited period and apply only to fish to be used for academic research or traditional rituals. In fact, permission comes not from the national government but from the prefecture, a local authority.

The imposition of these restrictions is a clear violation of the human rights of the Ainu, who are indigenous to Japan and who have a right to pass down our language, culture and traditions to future generations. If Ainu were allowed to harvest salmon freely, it would be possible to revive traditional food practices and fishing methods, aiding the transmission of the culture to our young

people. The legal basis for this can be found in Article 13 of the Constitution of Japan, the "Right to the Pursuit of Happiness," and in Article 27 of the "International Treaty on Civic and Political Rights," signed by Japan in 1979.

Finally, I pose the question "Who owns the salmon?" In nature, salmon swim freely through the oceans as they grow, returning after three or four years to the river of their birth to spawn. During their years in the ocean, they know no national boundaries. Human beings are the ones who create nations and then claim that marine products "belong" to them. We should not forget that all people of the world have a right to share natural marine resources. Of course, many other animals also depend on the bounty of nature, including creatures that survive on salmon, such as owls and many other species.

Human beings cannot afford to be arrogant. Nature protects humankind, but we cannot claim that humankind protects nature. After all, humankind is but one small part of the great natural world.

(Translated from Japanese.)

Shiro Kayano with his father, Shigeru Kayano, on the grounds of the Kayano Shigeru Nibutani Ainu Museum. November, 1997.

SHIRO KAYANO (Ainu) was born in Hokkaido, Japan in 1958 and currently lives in Nibutani Village, Biratori Township, where he is the Executive Director of the Biratori Nibutani Ainu Language School. The son of Ainu cultural leader Shigeru Kayano, Shiro graduated from Asia University in 1981 with a degree in law and went to work in the private sector. In 1987 he participated in a study tour to Canada, where his encounter with First Nations peoples inspired him to value his own identity as an Ainu.

Recognizing that a unique language is the key to the preservation of a people, he devoted himself to the Ainu language. Administering and expanding the language school has been his primary occupation since 1992. Shiro Kayano serves as deputy director of the Kayano Shigeru Nibutani Ainu Museum, and as chairman of the Ainu Language Pen Club. Founder of the *Ainu Language Quarterly*, he was featured in the 1993 film *Language Is the Soul of a People: Building a Boat*. In 1998, he announced his decision to run for a seat in the Diet of Japan. In all his activities, he devotes himself to promoting understanding of Ainu as a living language.

Shiro Kayano

GLORIA BIRD

Images of Salmon and You

Your absence has left me only fragments of a summer's run
on a night like this, fanning in August heat a seaweeded song.
Sweat glistens on my skin, wears me translucent, sharp as scales.

The sun wallowing its giant roe beats my eyes back red and dry.
Have you seen it above the highway ruling you like planets?
Behind you, evening is Columbian, slips dark arms

around the knot of distance that means nothing
to salmon or slim desiring. Sweet man of rivers,
the blood of fishermen and women will drive you back again,

appointed places set in motion like seasons. We are like salmon
swimming against the mutation of current to find
our heartbroken way home again, weight of red eggs and need.

Kettle Falls on the Columbia, Circa 1937

The river is a green crystalline ribbon flowing though the heart of the lands of the Inland Salish peoples. During the salmon run, the various bands flock to the river for sustenance, both water and salmon connected in the image of light dating back to ancient times when Coyote released Salmon from the first trap. The natural falls lie low and shimmer in the translucent green light that is the river. The falls form tables of water scallops in the fast running waters where the backs of salmon dapple the glistening surface. A thick forest surrounds the area. In the fall, just before the world turns a mottled green and the fog rolls in, the last of summer ignites across the hill backs.

We arrive in the fishing camp just before sunset. The colors along the river are subdued by the mist from the waterfall, barely three-hundred feet long, and on our side of the river, the rocks are pockmarked—or kettle-shaped—which gives us the name for this place, Kettle Falls. These gathering times bond us as kinsmen and fellow fishers among the people of the Inland. We are related by blood, by inter-tribal marriage and by the act of fishing for salmon. This year, there are many king salmon to be caught, and already the smell of smoked fish thickens the air and sets my stomach to growling. Only recently, we finished the last of the smoke-dried salmon that I made into a soup of salmon and dumplings, a staple meal through the long winter. The dried salmon can be stored in flour sacking and is packed easily because it weighs so little once dry. I look forward to tasting the fresh fish cooked outdoors again.

Our son, daughter-in-law and grandson are already at the fishing camp when we arrive, and the old campsite is alive with excitement. Men are at one end of the camp, gambling, women are talking and laughing in groups and children are playing. My son lives with his wife's family on the Colville Reservation on the other side of the river. This year, they made their camp on our side, which gives me an opportunity to visit with my grandson, Sussep, already a young man. Fifteen years earlier, I was present at his birth in the spring of flooding, and rocked him in my arms as if he were as fragile as a baby blue jay. I know he is no longer a child, and I must remember to keep my memories of his infant years to myself.

In the evening, my husband attends to his fishing gear, in particular, his spears with points of sharpened deer horn. He sets the deer horn to the frame with pine pitch,

Kettle Falls on the
Columbia River,
circa 1908.

working his way around each with care, checks his line, tying it to the head of his long-handled spear. Every night before retiring he goes through this process in preparation for another day's fishing. I watch him work while I cook our evening meal. He is patient and works with a steady hand. The low roaring of the falls is heard over the domestic sounds coming from nearby camps, familiar and comforting.

The flap of our teepee is pushed aside and our grandson Sussep enters. He clears the opening with the full energy of his youth and greets his grandfather and me. But as his eyes adjust to the dim light and he notes his grandfather working on his gear, his smile fades. "Grandpa, when will you ever change?" he asks.

Then he turns to me. "Grandma," he begs, "don't let him take those pieces of wood and bone to the river, he will embarrass me in front of the others." Hotness erupts on my cheeks. It seems as though the young nowadays can always find something wrong with the old ways, but it would not be good to argue the night before fishing. I look to my husband as he keeps working—as if he hadn't heard the pain in our grandson's voice, though I know he has. By way of reprimand, I tell my grandson about the time the whites rode through the fishing camp.

"They threw the bones of animals into the water, and the salmon left, do you remember that story?" The story was a recent event and made an impact that talking about Coyote didn't. Sussep nodded his head.

Fishing for the younger men is so different from the way it is with the older men. These younger ones skip from boulder to boulder along the shore, hoping to spear the salmon with their whiteman-made iron spears. It is the same in every camp where the old men work. The young are learning from the convenience of the metal-worked spears purchased from the whites to devalue the self-sufficient methods that our people's survival depends upon. It is a contention of the younger generation

Gloria Bird

50

that the handmade implements are not sophisticated enough for them. Sussep is no different. I feel a heavy loss of another piece in the chain of survival and I worry for him. I worry for us all.

Although we women are not allowed to go near the river while the men fish, we know what goes on. I knew that his father, our son, tried to get him out on the scaffolds but that Sussep was not able to stay above the raging falls for too long a time. The scaffolds shook above the thundering water. I also know that Sussep is as skittish as a rabbit when he is teased. Teasing is a way to aid in the shaping of behavior that our old people used in the old days, but I knew that Sussep reacts in anger. This seems

the only response of these young ones who were sent to the missionary school.

It is not my place to attempt to dissuade my husband from fishing the way our people have from the beginning. I refuse to come to the aid of my grandson. It was not good luck to have this youngster in the teepee complaining while his grandfather prepared his fishing gear. I ask why he has come. "The salmon leader will call the men out in the morning," he said. He left as he came with a *whoosh* of the teepee flap. He told us what we already knew, and I was struck by my grandson's lack. Later, when my husband was getting ready to sleep, I asked him why he would not use the metal spears. He smiled and told me that the young men could not spear as many fish as he, even with their new spears. He comes from a family of fishers, and it is true. He is a good fisherman.

The next morning, after the men leave, we women move to our work site. We pick a spot in the shade in which to work at slicing and smoking the salmon. The fishing season means long hours of working hard and the shade suits us well. We work efficiently and quickly. Everything depends on how the salmon are treated during the fishing season. If we do not follow all of the rules regarding their treatment, our teachings tell us that the fish will not return. It means that we follow the directions as they were passed down to us. This includes staying away from the water and taking care in the disposal of salmon innards. Even the children must follow the rules during fishing season.

I was contemplating the implications of my grandson's behavior of the previous night when a young girl moved next to me. She was the daughter of one of a visiting tribe's fishing leader—she was Spokane. She had large dark eyes, a shy girl. She greeted me as grandmother properly and she asked if I might help her. I thought she meant with cutting salmon, but when I looked at her, I sensed her inner turmoil and stopped

what I was doing. She was worried. She looked at the ground while she told me that on her way to catch up with the women that morning she had run out of her camp, trailing behind. She stopped to remove a pebble from the bottom of her moccasins, leaning against a tree to get her bearings. Too late, she realized that she had her hand on a fishing spear. I told her that since she did not do it intentionally it was not her fault. I could not ascribe blame to the girl who was very shaken by the accident. But I also knew that Indian taboo existed for a reason, and I was not as sure as I seemed. *Was it an older or a newer spear?* I should have, but dared not ask.

While we cut fish and lace the fillets onto stakes around the fire, conversations drift in and out of our hearing, carried on air from the river. I hear snatches of the young men making fun of the old ones' handmade spears and netting. In the old days, they would not have dared speak as disrespectfully to their old people as they do now, I thought, making fun. I knew Sussep loved his grandfather, but was confused by the belief that the white man's iron spears were superior. If it weren't for the ingenuity of our ancestors, we would not be here today. But I feel that the world is changing, too; I sense other disturbing changes coming in the near future. I

Gloria Bird

am not so sure that my husband and I will live to see those changes, and I fear them.

During the day, two girls, the daughters of one of our guests, are caught throwing scraps of fish gut at one another. It is a sure sign of the trouble to come, but I dismiss the thought. At noontime, the people are called for the distribution of the salmon. The salmon divider distributes the salmon equally among all of the people there, whether or not they were fishing. Everyone is given an equal portion. It could mean a period of starvation if we were stingy. I catch a glimpse of my husband briefly. He appears tired, yet he has the excited air of a younger man. He is a fisherman. The thought of the young girl tries to push into my consciousness, but I drive it back again. *Was it his?* After our noon meal, we go back to work.

There are times when, as an old woman, I have regretted very little. I have had a good life, and I have enjoyed traveling the way we Indians do, across the plains and over mountains in search of roots and berries, or with my husband to buy or trade for horses and other necessities. To fish. I regret that we did not take Sussep, our firstborn grandson, into our home, as is the old custom. When his parents settled in a square house on the reservation, they wanted him to

attend the mission school. I was saddened to see him grow into a man who did not seem to know anything about our people or our life. But that is in the past. I regret so few things from my long life, but that, I regret most—even over my silence that day.

As the women work, I hear the story about a woman who had salmon powers and who, it was said, was able to call salmon into her weir. *If this were possible, would it have changed the course of a young woman's life more recently? Was it possible for an ordinary young woman to touch the salmon spear?* Uneasy, remembering the young woman's dilemma, I begin humming an old children's feast song as I grasp the firm but slippery flesh of salmon after salmon. I slice from the backbone down following the outer edge of ribcage to the belly. The afternoon wears on and the women's foreheads glisten in the simmering heat. Soon the leaves would turn, and the nights would grow long. We would have salmon enough to last us the winter with more left over.

In the stories of long ago, Coyote was the first divider. I have heard that he jumped into the mouth of the giant beaver and cut his heart loose. He sliced the beaver to pieces and distributed the body parts to the animal people who were locked inside. The distribution of those parts became the present day

Spear fishing at either Kettle Falls or Celilo Falls.

and the salmon fillet I held down. I walk toward the men's voices muffled in the sounds of the waterfalls. Something has happened, but there is nothing to be done but wait. The women are all gathered together; none dare to close in any further. We are aware that the noise the men were making was sure to spook the salmon.

A younger man is running into the camp from the river, and we watch him come. As he searches our faces he must see expectant fear, then relief, as his eyes pass over one woman then the next without beckoning to any one. But when he turns his gaze on me, I feel my knees buckle. He motions for me to follow him down to the river. The men's trail veers from the larger trail that runs parallel to the banks. I'd never been on this trail during fishing season. Something out of the ordinary was happening, and because of it, fishing would be postponed, perhaps for days. I felt as if I was floating to the edge of the water.

I remember that particular day for many reasons. I remember that I thought it was my man and partner in this life who had an accident. The vision of living my life alone panned out before me. It would be many years before that would happen, but at that moment when I thought it was my man, I prepared for the worse. My heart raced like

Kalispel, Coeur d'Alene, Colville and Spokane peoples. This is how we are all related. I am old, but I remember hearing this story of creation that could very well have happened along this river, in this very spot, in the days when animals and humans communicated to one another.

In the late afternoon, when I hear yelling coming from the river, my heart freezes. It is unusual to hear shouting because the men did not talk much when fishing. All of the women looked in the direction of the rising voices coming from the river. I put my knife

Gloria Bird

a wild turkey in my chest, and I clutched my chest as if I could suppress the fear gathering there. But it was not my life partner; it was Sussep.

I learned later that Sussep was asked by his father to take his place on the scaffold above the river. What happened next, no one was sure of, only that as he leapt from the tenuous perch closer in to the shore, he lost his footing on the slippery rocks. When his body slid into the water, he grabbed a hemp rope that slid with him into the river. Somehow in his struggle to reach the shore, the rope tangled around his legs and arms. Men along the shore dove into the water to bring him out, my husband among them. Sussep regained consciousness later, and was well again in a few days' time. Only in his sleep would there be an indication, in the form of fitful dreams, that he'd nearly passed from our world into the next.

That was twenty years ago. Now, I live with my son and daughter-in-law in their house on the reservation. Things move so fast, and after my husband passed on, I had to give up the buckboard and horses. My son believed I was too old to ride a horse. I've adjusted to my new life, and it has been a blessing to me in my old age to have many good memories on which I may draw. Of our life before, of being free.

On that day long ago, the salmon fishing ceased. We believe that when flesh or remains of anything living is thrown into the water, the salmon take leave. And they did. For two days, we waited for their return. The divider was sent to the river each morning, and every day he returned empty-handed. I knew that it wasn't just that the men dove into the water, but that a woman was at the river, too. That woman was I. There were other incidents to be blamed as well. Too many times when there is fault it is larger than the individual, and I knew that a woman had touched a fishing spear. I thought about the children who threw the fish innards, and that they were not stopped. The younger people needed the adults to teach them. This was the necessity of working as a community; everyone did their part. I could have spoken to them, but even I had not.

The men and women sweated separately for two days, praying for the return of the salmon. In the old days, our lives depended upon the salmon, the berries, the deer and the roots. The seasons guided us, and with each new fruit of the earth we celebrated with meals for the offerings given to us, the Creator's children. We shared our food with one another as a community. All of those things depended upon our passing the customs and teaching on to the children. For those two days we all suffered, some of us with guilt. I knew that my silence made me complicit, or at least partly responsible. To compensate, since that time I have taken the role of grandmother to heart, and will always intervene when it comes to teaching the children.

The year was 1937, and as I have said, we did not know what the future held in store for us Indians. Maybe that is for the best. We did not know, for instance, that the following year would be our last for fishing for king salmon in the homeland streams. One thing about us is that we believed things would remain the same forever. For us, the span of time means from the first beginnings, when the animals talked, through the present day. For us, it was easy to believe everything would always remain the way it was because we trusted our stories. We knew that the salmon, berries and roots that we ate kept us strong and healthy. Back then, our diet was a balanced one that protected us from sickness. Our lives centered on the game, the fish and the indigenous plant life. The intimate knowledge of the landscape was survival knowledge. But in a single generation, all of that knowledge was nearly lost.

In 1939 the backwaters of Grand Coulee Dam flooded our beloved falls, but it was the building of Chief Joseph Dam that prevented the salmon from reaching our homelands and ended our way of life for good. We were required by the government to take up farming. I believe it was intended to keep us on the reservations because before that time we wandered freely across the country. My husband was not able to adjust to reservation life and I believe it was making that transition to farming that killed his spirit. I don't blame him for leaving. In a few more years' time, all of the land surrounding our reservations was covered over by wheat. Camas and bitterroot became harder and harder to find. For the roots and berries that we gathered, we were forced to ask for permission to gather from the whites in our own territory. Everything happened too fast for old people like me. Yet I still have my memories of what it was like for us before to comfort me.

The story of Coyote releasing Salmon from the first trap shifts and in the story as it is now told, Coyote will return to tear apart the dams that block the passage of the salmon. This time, it is the dams that are the monsters he will slay. Coyote will come back and rescue us again as he did in the old days. I wish he would hurry up and come.

Gloria Bird

Illusions

There are no illusions to be had
in the aftermath of flooding dams,
like love. My vision of that silver leaping
and flesh so red it appeared raw
and bleeding was the consequence
of bad medicine threatening
every living thing on the planet,
manifesting itself today in mental
images of man-made concrete
blocks, cold and infertile.

And so you are, lost to any saving
graces, a vacant, pitiful soul
who can neither tell the difference between
love flooding like a salmon run on a good day
nor stilted indifference. There is no good
to come from disrespect of the body of salmon
in which both water and light mean
the same thing and signify to those
who need both that the story is far
from being over.

Kalispel fishermen
at *Si-si-ah* Creek on
the Pend Oreille
River, 1908.

GLORIA BIRD (Spokane) is a member of the Spokane Tribe of Indians of Washington State and grew up on both the Spokane and Colville Indian Reservations. She is one of the founding members of the Northwest Native American Writers Association. She received her M.A. from the University of Arizona in Tucson and her B.A. from Lewis & Clark College in Portland, Oregon.

Ms. Bird is the author of the poetry collections *Full Moon on the Reservation,* which won the Diane Decorah First Book Award for Poetry, and most recently, *The River of History: Prose Poems.* She is an associate editor for the *Wicazo Sa Review,* a Native literary magazine and has served as the contributing literature editor for *Indian Arts Magazine.* She has been included in many anthologies and has written introductions to *Dancing on the Rim of the World,* with Elizabeth Woody, and *Writing the Circle: Native Women of Western Canada.*

With Joy Harjo she co-edited the anthology *Reinventing the Enemy's Language: North American Native Women's Writing* and has been active in encouraging Native women writers. In her introduction to that anthology she talks about the task of the writers to use the English language to "turn the images around to mirror an image of the colonized to the colonizers as a process of decolonization. . . ."

After years of teaching in various schools including the Institute of American Indian Arts in Santa Fe, she is back in Spokane, Washington, where she lives with her three children and works as a grants writer for the Spokane Indian Tribe. She is currently writing a collection of fiction and essays as well as completing a manuscript of poetry based on the testimony of women and children during the Nez Perce Retreat of 1877.

Gloria Bird

Mieko Chikappu

Salmon Coming Home in Search of Sacred Bliss

Translated by
Jane Corddry Langill
with Rie Taki and
Judith Roche

The salmon come riding home
Home from long journeys through the great seas
How magnificent they flash!
Look, home is just ahead, up there
Push on a little more.
Weaving the waves together, the salmon
Dance in small, joyful jumps
Scales shine a bright silver.
Riding the rhythm of the breaking waves,
They twist their bodies and leap!

But it does not always go as well as hoped.
Twice and three times they jump, and again.
Exhausted, some become swallowed by waves,
Where they crest on sandy shore
Weakly, twice, three times, they try to jump again
And finally fall back where they lie.
Awaiting them, the gulls and the crows,
Their ordeal fated from time beyond time.
Yielding to the resistance of the river
The salmon come riding home
To their birth place, home,
To their precious motherland.

This is the river that sent them off to sea,
This home from where they emerged

Young Mieko with
her mother near
Lake Akan.

Home river, resisting, not holding them back
Whispers promises of life.

The crashing waves of the river
Never troubled with such matters,
Break on the shore again and again, unchanging.
Only those who catch the rhythm of these waves
Will last to create life anew.

Ride the waves and jump!
Ahh, a splendid leap!
Yes, you will be fine now
You have made it through the hardest part.
Now you need only swim home, swift now
For home is just up there, just ahead.

As salmon go home to their mother, the river,
The river goes home to its mother, the mountain
And in the home mountains
Reside the wisdom and teachings of the ancestors.
Maku-Ta-Fuchi (Ekashi), ancestors
Deep mountain-dwelling—grandmothers (grandfathers).
Our ancestors, ancients dwelling deep in the mountains,
our progenitor gods, the guardian deities.
The mountains, the breasts of mother earth.
The rivers that flow there,
The mother's milk of mother earth,
Take from the mountain-dwelling ancients
Full measure of nurture
To nourish the salmon.
The salmon following
The familiar scent and taste
Ride the river home.

Aflame with the crimson color of marriage, the salmon
Seek their lovers.
For the salmon, the act
Spinning out life
Is an act of death.
For the salmon
Life lives in death.
The salmon bets its life on love,
Beautiful evanescent ceremony,
Bodies pressed together on the river bed.
Lovers push each other's passion
Until it hurts.
Pure, straight love for survival.
The single act of love
Risks all.
The salmon die
Ahh, so tenderly.

Mieko Chikappu's mother, Fude, playing the *mukkuri*, an Ainu mouth harp.

Mieko Chikappu

So fiercely flames their passion,
They love each other to death
In transcendent moment of ultimate bliss.
To perform this sacred ceremony of love
The salmon ride the river home.

Now, cradled in the arms of home,
You may rest
For you will live on
In the memories of your children
You will endure forever
So rest well, now
Kamuy chep
Oh, most sacred fish!

(Translated from Japanese.)

Detail of a mat woven by Mieko Chikappu with traditional design patterns.

MIEKO CHIKAPPU (Ainu), born
in Hokkaido in 1948, takes her name as
an artist from *chikap*, the Ainu word for
bird. She is a poet, writer, activist and
embroidery artist specializing in Ainu
motifs and is widely considered a leader
among Ainu women of her generation.
She was trained by her mother in traditional Ainu woman's culture, including
embroidery and dance. In 1964 she was
the heroine of the film, *Yukar no Sekai, Aki
no Seikatsu* (World of the Epics, Life in
Autumn). She has been active in the
cause of minority and indigenous
peoples, participating in summits, exchanges and conferences around the
world. She has also produced concerts
of ethnic music.

Her embroidery work has been ex-
hibited in museums and galleries, including the National Museum of Folk Art,
and a widely acclaimed 1992 exhibition
of her work toured New York, San Fran-
cisco and Los Angeles in conjunction
with a conference of indigenous peoples
of Japan and the United States.

She has published many poems,
books and articles about Ainu culture
and embroidery and is also in demand as
a reporter and essayist for newspapers
and magazines. In addition to her numerous articles and poems, her major
publications include *Kaze no Megumi: Ainu
Minzoku no Bunka to Jinken* (Blessings of
the Wind: the Culture and Human
Rights of the Ainu People), *Ainu Moshir:
Ainu Minzoku kara Mita Hoppo Ryodo
Henkan Kosho* (Peaceful Land of the
People: the Ainu Perspective on Nego-
tiations for Return of the Northern Territories), *Ainu Monyo Shishu no Kokoro*
(The Spirit of Ainu Embroidery Patterns), *Chikappu Mieko Ainu Monyo Shishu
Sakuhinshu* (The Ainu Embroidery of
Mieko Chikappu: Collected Works),
and *Gendai Nihon Bunkaron: Watakushi to
wa Nani ka* (A Theory of Contemporary
Japanese Culture: So What Am I?).

Mieko Chikappu

ELIZABETH WOODY

Tradition with a Big "T"

The monotony of work for the tribes, even the gossip run-through two or three times on the Rez, was too much for Elly. She did not feel her usual exhilaration about the summer ahead. It looked as if it was going to be the same old "same old." When Jasper called to ask her to come visit at his mother's place next to the Columbia River, she agreed it was time to take a small break. Eloise was not sure what it meant to be "on the river."

"Fishing?" Bobbi said, making it sound high in tone, without the *g* on the end, "Yeah, I like fishing." They were walking over the bridge toward the store. They had walked countless times over this bridge. The peach T-shirt accentuated the rich, milky brown quality of Bobbi's early outdoor summer complexion. She eventually became so brown she looked finely dusted like a light and dark elk.

"Gill netting, Bobbi. He's a big time fisherman. He takes his fish around and sells it or trades. Our great uncle used to fish with a dip net at Celilo and sell the fish right there or to Seufert's cannery." Her sister looked interested, but felt irritated. It was not necessary to explain everything to her. Bobbi smiled and waved at a passing car. As a group, the occupants chanted, "Bobbi! Bobbi!"

"I know what that means—like Mowitch does at Shears." She kicked a rock against the cement railing of the bridge. The small chink was the emphasis she added for her annoyance. Bobbi was always defensive over her Nana's big-sister-know-it-all tones. They grew up in the same house, after all. "It's tradition with a big 'T', on the Big River."

Pausing to look over the rail at the creek below, and thinking of their cousin, she changed the subject. "Do you think Mowitch really was visited by Bigfoot?"

"I don't know. He thinks so. If you smelled something stinky, like he said he did, what would you think?"

"I'd think someone was being mean and throwing rotten eggs at my camp." Bobbi's face caught a light from the water. Her rounded face had high cheek bones. The reflected morning light on her face made her look like an angel picture. Bobbi's hair shone with reddish highlights from the sun's gleam. The swept-up and curled-back bangs added some height to her small body.

Bobbi giggled and her eyes curled up at the ends. This pushed her long eyelashes up, like a Kewpie doll. This and the tinkle of the giggle made Eloise laugh, too.

"Oh, who'd do such a thing to Mowitch? He can be bad, sometimes, but he minds his own business. He's a loner, unless he drinks."

"Yeah, he's alone too much, out there at Shears Bridge. Maybe it's a girl Bigfoot." Bobbi giggled again and continued. "Since he can't see her at night, she has to wave her perfume at him."

Eloise laughed with her head thrown back, thinking of their handsome cousin courted by a homely Bigfoot. Her hair touched the small of her back. The short T-shirt, that said 'Trucking,' revealed a thin stripe of cream-yellow skin, and a small roll of fat moved over the top of her jeans. Eloise didn't wear cutoffs, unless she went swimming. The sun burned her too easily.

She said hurriedly, "Let's go. The bus will be up at the highway soon. If we miss it, we'll have to resort to hitchhiking." They both knew their family would chastise them for even thinking of doing so. It was not an option, even though they saw hippies with their thumbs out passing through the reservation on US 26. Eloise put a knuckle into her sister's arm with her thumb up, for emphasis. Bobbie wrinkled her finely bridged nose at her bossy sister.

"Wait," Bobbi said, as she bent over and picked up the small gravel rock and heaved it out over the creek. The splash made a small crater in the rolling surface of the creek. "For good luck. See how fine that shape was." Bobbi always had some sign or statement for good thoughts. A carry over from their *Kuthla* (maternal grandmother), who watched for some sign of encouragement—a bird talking, or the way the wind moved seemed to agree with her. Eloise was not so, well, superstitious.

❧

The wind was strong and blew Mowitch's hair loose from under the small leather cap pulled tightly over the thick short hair on his crown. His hair, cut into long layers on the sides, feathered back smoothly into crow wings. Sitting on a camp stool over the rolling and wild water of the falls, he took in the wind. Smells were absent in the ferocity of the wind. Occasionally, he smelled the fish guts behind him, the live fish coating in the drying slime around him and in his gunny sack. There was the sweet scent of heated sage and grasses above him and the dirt essence of the rocks all around him.

Upriver, he could hear the loud voices of some tourists snapping photos of the scaffolds across the way. They needed to talk loudly over the water. The thunder of the falls was everywhere in your head. Mowitch didn't need to talk and when he did, it was never loud. The whiteness of the falls accumulated a light of its own, occasionally veiled with small rainbows. The chutes of the small streams that fed into the larger Shears Falls seemed like the small wisps of hair blowing around its face.

His partner was with his mother lifting up *pia-xī* (bitterroot) from the fields in a lesser wind under the same clear sun. The wind was a constant on the land. He could imagine them, bent over the slight and sturdy *kuupan* (digging sticks), colorful bandannas on their heads. With the slight bend in the *kuupan* and its point, they made a small gap around the plant, lifting the root from the soil so the only disturbance was a small hole. Carefully, they shook the bags to level the *pia-xī* to place the new one in the small *wapa'as* (root bags, sally bags) tied to their waists. Bev looked up now, in the direction of Shears Bridge, and smiled. Her sunglasses rose with the smile on her cheeks. Mowitch felt good seeing this.

She told him once, "They never make sunglasses right for my face. And, when they do, *evverrybuddy* has them, around here."

Mowitch looked at her smooth face. "Is that because everybody around here has a round face?"

She snapped his shoulder with her fingertips, a light touch by any comparison. Pretending to be exasperated, Bev retorted, "Oh, you!"

Mowitch pretended to duck and rubbed the shoulder she touched. Bev was kind to him. He was kind to her in return. He couldn't help himself. He liked teasing her. She was serious about everything. They were partners who worked this land for the good of their families and themselves. She was digging roots primarily for their elders, this time. Whatever became surplus was theirs to dry and store. His mom liked younger company, so it seemed Bev spent more time with mom than with him.

Mowitch felt movement in his net. Holding the dipping pole in his grip, a strength came up from his feet as he rose. To remain firmly on the platform, he had to will his connection to surface

Elizabeth Woody

there, on those two points. He used the safety rope sometimes. Sometimes, he didn't. Mowitch's awareness of others stopped instantly with his fisher's focus on the fish and his part in its life. The river's whiteness is a field of potential. He knew intimately the power in his net and held his breath in the next few moments. The fish, spirited and wild, looked at him, the eye tilting his way and away to the whiteness. Mowitch knew this salmon was as wild as he. Both had the same fight. Mowitch was oblivious to the people running over the volcanic rocks in his direction. Their cameras masked their faces. He felt his feet, his hands and the fish. The spring run would feed his family and the Longhouse. Since they gave thanks the year before, the *nusoox* returned and the people lived to catch them.

❧

Elly asked her sister, Bobbi, to take a few days off work and come with her. The thought of going to the Columbia River seemed cool, in more ways than one. Bobbi's interest was obvious, since she was a natural type. Bobbi loved anything to do with tradition and animals. She sincerely liked elderly people and their stories. The elders relished time spent with her. She visited equally with every-

one. Once, she wanted to adopt baby bats who lost their mothers in power lines that criss-crossed the Northwest from the dams and nuclear power plants. The call for adoption came over the evening news. As an endangered species they needed help. Wrapped in small white blankets with a small bottle in their mouths, they appealed to Bobbi. She decided not to volunteer, unable to persuade anyone to be a daytime bat-sitter. Their dad told her taking care of wild orphans was serious business. Her sister was tender-hearted.

Bobbi traveled well. She always fell instantly asleep. Her head lolled over to Elly's shoulder. Elly looked out of the window at the countryside as it passed. She loved rising from the canyon to Sidwalter Flats. The mountains all came into view. The old and small hills to the right, Mutton mountains and the young string of strong mountains posed on the left. Oregon's Cascade Range had the Three Sisters, Round Butte, Mount Washington, Bald Peter, Mount Jefferson and Mount Hood. In between the two mountain ranges were placid old junipers, sage and bunch grass. They would soon approach Hood and become immersed in the timber. It was strange how people called the trees *timber* or *wilderness*. The trees were slender second and third growth, excluding those on the reservation. Her *Kuthla* called it all "mountains." She said it like two words, "Mowwn-tins." Elly floated over the plains in reverie.

It was the shadow of the overhanging trees on the highway that made Elly drowsy, past Government Camp. This is where she lost interest in the roadside as it turned into roadside shops, eventually farmland, and people rushing back and forth. Some travelers with gear for camping rushed to the camp grounds. Others, the country tourists, rushed on their way to the big city for business and shopping.

Going to the city made her fill with excitement. Her parents had lived there with Eloise and her brother, Merlin, before their sister, Roberta, was born. She attended day school. Her father worked first as a welder on the bridges, then in the shipyards. Her mother worked for the state. Even their grandfather worked as a blacksmith in the shipping yards for a brief time. She had some relatives there. They shopped, went out to eat at hokey Chinese-American restaurants, saw movies and sat in velvety seats. They went to the zoo and fed everything peanuts or to OMSI (the Oregon Museum of Science and Industry). At the science center they walked through the giant Human Heart or tested their hearing, comparing the frequency they heard with other animals on the chart. Merlin claimed he could hear it all. This ability works well for him as a mechanic, listening to each car's engine. As a kid he could identify each visitor by their approaching vehicle.

Childhood memories of going alongside the mountains meant three things: Portland, The Dalles or Yakima. They went to Wapato to visit her great-uncle and his wife Edna, whom everyone adored. She was so matter-of-fact. This pleased and tickled everyone. One aunt called their great-aunt's manner "dry humor." The expression frequently used was "she calls a spade a spade." Great-Uncle was a wild-flying ace pilot and once Edna eased herself back among a group of sunning rattlesnakes on the airstrip in order to safely guide her husband down in his plane. Nothing fazed Edna after being married for years to Great-Uncle.

This time, they would only pull into the suburbs to meet up with Jasper. They rode the bus as far as Fairview. Approaching the first stop light, Bobbi woke up and stretched a good cat stretch. She said, as she always does, "Gee, I almost fell asleep."

Jasper Wallulluwit lived near the river in a trailer lot. Eloise met him when she suffered through her first term at the university. She was homesick in the city

Elizabeth Woody

if she stayed too long. Jasper, being a Yakama, understood her longing. He drove her to Warm Springs a few times when she felt bad.

The parking lot filled with expectant people. Jasper was back by the wall of the small bus stop. The people whirled in and out of a mass to retrieve their bags beside the bus. A peculiar stink from Camas across the river blew in from the mills. Eloise and Bobbi had their day packs shouldered and Eloise smiled her most brilliant and wide smile as she introduced Bobbi to Jasper. Jasper said, making the z's sound rich and smooth, "Just call me Jazz."

He wore a billed hat with the stitched yellow-gold words that said "Columbia" in a field of rich blue, a wind breaker, T-shirt and jeans. Basketball shoes were the only pretentious aspect to his clothing. His high tops were expensive. He had short hair, nearly the same color as Bobbi's. Their grandfather used to say that particular color was Yakama. Rich browns that darkened and highlighted in a wonderful way. Behind Jasper's back, Bobbi made her eyebrows go up and down as she looked at Elly. Elly deftly elbowed her with a subtle move only sisters can accomplish.

As the car, an older Lincoln, eased into the eastward freeway traffic, Jasper talked nonstop. He kept glancing at Eloise, who rode shotgun, and at the rear view mirror, at Bobbi. He liked Bobbi. At sixteen, she was beginning to enjoy adult interaction more. She was smiling and combing her bangs. Elly knew she was preening, being coquettish, for Jazz. Glimpsing the river, she thought it looked very smooth today, like his voice. Occasionally they passed a barge going upriver as they rode in the shadow of the volcanic and rough sides of the gorge. Sprays of springtime waterfalls appeared, now and then. Jasper told them about the winter. Sometimes, it was hard to drive home on the black ice, as if they were foreign to this country.

"Well, I'm preaching to the choir," he stopped his description of the winter road conditions. Then he said, "I have never stopped learning about this place. Last term, I took a class on geology. It interests me to think of what this place may have looked like a long time ago. Our people had the life."

The drive calmed Eloise. She said, "I don't really know much about this place, except the stories of Celilo Falls, and little at that. It made our mom too sad, except the kid's stuff. You know, riding back and forth on those hanging cable cars, feeling the spray, watching the rainbows that were little circles inside one another, coming out of the falls and the water's smell. She only had happy memories of Celilo. My aunt told me one time that she loved the town of Rowena. She was sad about losing Grandma and went there one day to think. She sat on the ground and looked around and right next to her was a *xumpsĩ* (wild celery). All those years she could never tell a *xumpsĩ* from the other hollow one, and she found a *xumpsĩ* that day! She picked and ate it. She told me she knew Grandma was a part of her, then."

Jazz shifted his body, intent on her words. After polite quietness, he spoke. "I remember my *Kuthla* saying that my father was a good provider. She packed four fish at a time on her back up the hill to clean them. When I looked at pictures of those old-time fish, so big and fat from the ocean, she easily packed over two hundred pounds."

Eloise quipped, "No wonder we have such strong and broad shoulders!"

"Good legs, too!" Bobbi chimed in, from the back seat.

"Can't argue about that. I like those qualities," Jasper said with a smile.

Eloise and Bobbi felt a surge of pride. All the older women at home were strong. They were strong. It was sad to be weak and lazy, pitiable. It seemed people were getting lazy and helpless, away from the land. Lives were becoming static. That wasn't just the Indian people, but everyone. The life of being in the right place at the right time was one of constant movement. In movement, they worked hard and with purpose.

❦

Jasper's mother's place seemed quiet with real wood paneling and trees all around the house. There were two sheds, one big, the other small and rough. The large freezer in the big shed was a real blessing, Jasper told them. The smaller drying shed his family always filled for trade. Old vehicles neatly parked in a line resembled a used car lot. These vehicles probably all ran smoothly. Jasper and his brothers built the place. Jasper showed them the way to their room.

It was late afternoon and a note from Jasper's sister said there would be a big dinner to meet his friends. Their mother was in Toppenish. Eloise looked at pictures that must be of his mother and sister. His mother looked young. There were several pictures of people. There were older black-and-white photos and the usual kids' school shots. People resembled one another. Jasper had lots of relatives.

"I'm assuming you both swim," Jasper

71

said. This caused both sisters to laugh. Of course both could swim. "We should go for a ride while it's still calm and light."

They walked down to the bank where there was a dock. Neatly folded nets with floaters and weights were hanging over whatever was available. A boat waited looking like a fine horse tied up and eager to go. It appeared easy as Jazz loaded them on, readied the boat and started the motor. He assumed the wheel and with authority headed to the center of the river. It was so brilliant away from the trees of the house. The world circled them as they turned and pointed into the waves. The waves had been indiscernible from the shore. Out in the open, the waves seemed to reach for the gold, brown and deep green land and point to the sky. Bobbi held her hair back as they gathered speed. She pointed to Eloise's earrings, "Like fish scales."

Eloise's abalone earrings were light and round on silver hoops. They flapped against her neck in the wind. Eloise reached back, looped her hair and tied it into a knot close to her head. Bobbi loved the efficient way Elly took care of her long hair.

Eloise looked up at the sky and saw the moon. She showed Bobbi. "Look, a day moon. Good luck, maybe. It will be a *dark* night filled with lots of stars."

Bobbi looked surprised at Elly's comment. Then, she glanced at Jasper's strong slender back, and to El's face, which shone like the moon they admired the moment before. They broadly smiled and the wind dried their exposed upper gums and chilled their front teeth. They laughed loud and uncontrollably when both their upper lips remained stuck above their teeth. Jasper beamed at them as the boat bounced over the waves. He thought they were laughing about the bouncing.

Bobbi leaned over to her sister's ear and said, with joy lightening her tone, "He's a really good person. I'm glad you brought me along."

The hills looked like the baskets they had seen in their grandparent's house. The color and design of the baskets and the hill's design made by gravity and eruptions were the same. The boat circled slowly and stopped moving, altogether.

Jazz turned to look at Eloise, saying with a mysterious quality, "This is about the place where we capsized once." Both sisters remained quiet. Bobbi's head snapped slightly to lock her eyes on him, deer-like. "We pulled up on a big wave. Nothing we could do. Another bunch stopped their boat and picked us up, one by one. My bro' wasn't to be found. I thought, 'Oh God, not now. He wasn't going to die in the *Nch'I-Wana*. No way!' So I dove back in. The others watched while I disappeared under the water. It was eerie. The only time in my short life, I felt frightened to the bone.

"The light seemed bright. I could see the rim of the boat, and swam around it. He could've been tied up or caught. I didn't see him. Then, I saw his legs. He was *in* the boat. Surfacing, I told them, 'He's in there. I don't know if he's all right.' Ollins looked hard at me. He had more years on the river.

"Later he said, 'A person could be knocked out in such an accident, then, that's all she wrote. There is too much to think about in a time like that. Worry's no good compared to praying. You don't think the worst until it's over.'

"Under again, I swam down and pulled up in the boat. There he was. He was in shock, sort of treading water in a pocket of air. He wasn't going to move. I tried to touch him, but he pushed me away. I said, 'Johnny, you've swam 'cross this river twice, just showing off. You can make it under this rim and come up a free man. I've done this once already, right now. I will do it again.' It was cold.

I knew he was suffering from the cold and shock."

In the excitement of the story, Bobbi innocently asked, "Did he make it?"

"Yeah, I pulled a quick one. I grabbed his waist and tugged him along. The others grabbed him when we came up. Anyone who's part of this river will do what is instinctual. He held his breath and is a strong swimmer, himself."

"Does he still fish?"

Jasper looked painfully out over the river. "No, some guys broke all his fingers one night. Took a baseball bat to his hands. He does carpentry some, but mostly he manages the paperwork, now."

Bobbi's back shot up straight, "Who would do such a thing? Why? Didn't you call the police?"

"People are hard on us, Bobbi." Jasper paused, overcome with emotion. Still, these young women caught everything without need for explanation or providing every detail.

"There's a man down some ways here who can tell you wonderful stories about why we should be on the Big River. He can tell you about the old days and the ones to come. The story is sad about having to leave our place here and how it's brought us down. The River is a playground." He stopped, swallowed a

73

Elizabeth Woody

bit of his thoughts, and continued. "We represent something that will never end, until the fish stop running. There are people in the government who want us to be gone forever. That's because they don't understand our purpose."

Bobbi leaned closer, "I hear that we were put on the land to care for it."

Jazz nodded, "Our very being, your being here, means the land has meaning and is sacred. Not in a holy spirituality, either. Words brought to us from the songs tell us that we need to practice our beliefs. When the fish are gone, we'll be gone—that's the end of life as we know it. People think stopping us will stop the progression of what is to come. I'm certain the people who broke my brother's hands thought they were doing right."

"No!" Eloise interjected, "They couldn't have. That's cruel. Any cruelty is downright evil."

Jasper sighed, "The origin of evil is in the conflicts of people."

Bobbi, visibly horrified, and not fazed by their university ideas, said, "That does not make it right."

Jasper looked at her, with intense eyes and a calm expression, "We brought ourselves problems by chang-ing our thinking. People are foolish by nature. Our minds can do anything, though. The old man I spoke of said

that once. He's a *Twatī*, an Indian doctor. He's also a radical."

"I don't believe in radicals. Those AIM people talk about places far away from us," Eloise said. "He can't be like that. If he's an Indian doctor, he has to be true to his vision, not the vision of others." She didn't know why she said that. Sometimes, she said things that were not really her own thoughts, but from some place secret or hidden within her. She knew she had to ask her mother about this *Twatī*. Hearing the conviction in her voice, she stopped herself, and said, "I'm sorry about your brother, is all. I don't know about the other people. I am assuming they weren't Indian. Still, a friend once told me to never assume, it makes an *ass* out of *u* and one out of *me*. I'm tired of hearing about hateful people. They don't make any sense to me."

Jasper smiled, "Does it matter who they were, or what they were? The root of the word radical means being at the source of life. This is too serious. I'm full of stories today. You two make me want to tell everything. I should've just taken you to the old man. He makes you feel peace, like the gentle wave we are on now. He tells stories much better than I can."

On the way back, Bobbi lifted up from her seat. She braced her tennis shoes on the floor and her shoulders on the seat to form an arch. She reached in her pocket. She pulled out a small blood-red rock and tossed it into the water. Eloise watched and wondered if Bobbi was looking for an answer or making a small sacrifice. That was her favorite rock.

She looked at Eloise and smiled, "This is still our home. I just rearranged a part of it with a bit of myself. Someday, I will come back here and find another to keep me company."

Eloise looked at Bobbi's face framed with her snapping hair, leaping in its richness like a fire. She was a good listener and probably would ask one of her elder friends about this day. Jasper was looking out over the river, intent on taking them to shore and dinner. He had caught salmon the day before and had driven all the way into Fairview to meet them. The waves glinted behind her. The trees moved behind them. The hills beamed heat in the angled sun. The sky would soon be rose. She felt as if she knew all this, without having to remember. Maybe it was the smell of the river. It seemed to have a scent all its own.

Their grandfather told her, "All water is connected, from below to the sky. All the rivers lead to one place, and that is what is inside you. You can never be lost, just follow a stream to bring you home. Baby, you belong to everyone and they belong to you. If you use water to heal yourself, to blend with life, you will no longer feel alone. Crying tells you the heart is strong enough for you to continue. You can still feel and show that is so, by water."

Gone a long time, now, this instruction to her as a child helped her through her grandfather's imminent death. She had no idea of his true intent, until this moment. Eloise had tears in her eyes, and thought it must have been the wind. She was not sure. Within the hour she would be laughing in an uproar after dinner. Salmon always made her feel happy.

Elizabeth Woody

TWANAT, to follow behind the ancestors

Along the mid-Columbia River are Celilo Indian Village and Celilo Park. On the right side of the freeway heading east is a peaked roof Longhouse and a large metal building. The houses in the village are older and you can miss them completely at a glance. You can sometimes see nets and boats beside the homes. Some houses are empty. By comparison, the park is frequently filled with lively and colorful wind surfers. This is above a place presently under the river, Celilo Falls, or *Wyam*.

Wyam means the "Echo of Falling Water" or "Sound of Water upon the Rocks." It was one of the most significant fisheries on the Columbia River system, the fourth largest North American waterway. In recent decades the greatest irreversible change occurred in the middle Columbia as the site was inundated by The Dalles Dam on March 10, 1957. The drop in elevation of the river from its origin to the Pacific makes it a powerhouse. This is part of the reason for the construction of the dams to convert the strength in its velocity into cheap electricity. The obvious effects we experience now seemed insignificant in the boom of construction and employment of that time.

Glaciers in an extreme meltdown cut a path with torrential water through the volcanic land after the last ice age. This formed, in part, the Columbia River Gorge and Celilo Falls. This dramatic formation has given us a beautiful land that some compare to Hawaii in the more humid, wet sections. The fiery upheavals of the area described from geological study show us this is a land of cataclysmic change.

Historically, the *Wyampum* lived at *Wyam* for over 12,000 years. The estimates vary, but *Wyam* is one of the longest continuously inhabited communities in North America. Estimates will always vary as our tenure in the Western Hemisphere is disputed due to changes in the belief system of the stolid science of archeology. The elders tell us we have been here from time immemorial.

Today we know Celilo Falls as more than a lost landmark. It was a place as revered as one's own mother. The story of *Wyam*'s life is the story of the salmon, and my own

that nestled below the petroglyph, She-Who-Watches or *Tsagaglallal*. My grandmother, Elizabeth Thompson Pitt (*Mohalla*), was a *Wyampum* descendent and a *Tygh* woman. My grandfather, Lewis Pitt (*Wa Soox Site*), was a *Wasco*, *Wishram* and *Watlala* man. Epidemics of influenza and malpractice by doctors of the day were at fault. My grandparents lived through this due to Indian medicine—part spirit, native herbs and chemistry. What stories I have inherited include this medicine as an emotional cornerstone in their lives. The strength they had to acquire at a young age is what guided them through all the losses that followed.

(above)
Elizabeth Woody
at the petroglyph,
She-Who-Watches,
or *Tsagaglallal*.

(right)
Charlotte Edwards Pitt,
Elizabeth Woody's
great-grandmother.

ancestry. I live with the forty-year absence and silence of Celilo Falls, much as an orphan lives hearing of the kindness and greatness of his or her maternal parent.

I use this metaphor of mother, because both my grandparents lost their parents at a young age. The original locations of my ancestral villages on the *Nch'I-Wana* (Columbia River) are Celilo Village and the *Wishram* village

Elizabeth Woody

Adaptation is necessary for survival. Despite the need for change, old lessons are not ignored by choice. We have abided by natural law for thousands of years. Our civilization did not detrimentally impact resources because of this. In our world view, everything has a life and purpose on the earth. There is a reason for everything, while we may not always understand why. It is not a simple platitude but a cultural life way.

This is how I view my experiences with loss and how I have learned about the cultural life of the Columbia River Plateau. My connections to Celilo Falls are tenuous at best. I was born two years after Celilo drowned in the backwaters of The Dalles Dam. The tribal people who gathered there did not believe it possible.

My people have not talked much of Celilo. The grief is so great. What I did hear were small bits and pieces. Chief Tommy Kuni Thompson was one of the chiefs who negotiated with the U.S. Army Corps of Engineers in that time. He "exhorted Congress to prevent the closing" of the gates of the dam. "The Almighty took a long time to make this place," he said. As the backwaters grew to the falls, he held a sing. Martha Ferguson McKeown in *Welcome to Our Salmon Feast* said he never spoke of salmon in English. Salmon were a gift from the Creator and sacred.

My grandmother was a Thompson. Her father was James Thompson (*Wa-ta-hus*). She told us that Chief Tommy Thompson was her uncle. Chief Thompson's reasoning is more significant to me than deliberations of Congress, as it determined the destiny of the people who lived along the great river. People followed their leaders through acclimation. Leaders deliberated issues through careful thought and input from their villages. Most American citizens in the country, however, felt the construction of the dams was necessary.

My grandfather fished at Celilo with his brother, George Pitt II, at a site a relative or friend permitted, as is their privilege. They fished on scaffolds above the white water with a dip net. Since locations are inherited, they probably did not have a spot. They were

Chief Tommy Thompson and his wife, Flora, at the last salmon feast at Celilo Falls, 1956.

A network of cables with basket ferries transported Native people to their favorite fishing rocks at Celilo Falls on the Columbia River.

Wascopum, not *Wyampum*. Catching a fish, the fisher hollered, "HO!" They would lift up the dip net with its wild, powerful fish. My mother and aunt, Charlotte and Lillian, recall riding the dangerous cable cars back and forth over the white water of the falls. This, I imagine, was to my great-uncle's place. Andrew David (*Tuutawaĩsa*) fished on Big Island. My uncle, Lewis, who was preschool age, recalls the hot sands and the indescribable smell of the falls. A smell that he cannot find to compare or show me today.

When the fish ran, people were wealthy. People from all over the country would come to Celilo to watch the "Indians" catch fish. They would buy the fish freshly caught. It was one the most famous tourist sites in North America. You can tell a native Oregonian or Washingtonian by the accuracy of their fond memories of Celilo Falls. Today my uncle tells me one can identify a true Northwesterner by their love for the salmon. What happened at *Wyam* was more significant than entertainment. People gathered here by season through

Elizabeth Woody

multi-millennium generations to catch *nusoox* and news of relatives across the river or far away. People celebrated their happiness with horse racing and gambling. Women played card games like *Wa-look-sha* and *Montee* in their free time. People played stick games in the evenings.

During the day women cleaned large amounts of finely-cut fish and hung the parts to dry in the heat of the arid landscape. We ate all of the fish, except for the guts. Nutritionally complete, the fish provided essential nutrients, dried or fresh. Coupled with the fruits and roots, the diet was high in calcium, iron, vitamin C, healthy oils and minerals. Before the building of the dams upriver, the fishers caught June hogs. These salmon were unbelievably large and fat for their long journey to distant spawning grounds. I have heard of women

Women playing a gambling game at the last Celilo Falls salmon feast, 1956.

who packed these fish four at a time, while dragging the tails on the ground behind them. Imagine one seventy-pound fish and then imagine carrying four of them up a hill. The people were healthy and strong from the natural diet and lifestyle.

The enormous quantity of spawning fish running to the various tributaries, some as far north as Canada, could feed a whole family through the winter. *Chah-lī*, finely pounded dried flesh of the salmon mixed with dried berries, could store for up to two years. Expertly cut, dried salmon flesh in drying sheds looked like spread kites. The women dried the heads and gills. The spines and tails, with small orange windows of dry flesh between the bones, went into soup, eventually. Many had enough to trade with other tribes or individuals for specialty items. We had Klickitat baskets from such trades. My grandfather's mother, Charlotte Edwards Pitt (*Y-yuten*), traded her fine pictorial beadwork, for example.

No one would starve if they could work. Even those who could not physically work had some talent that they could share. It was a dignified existence. Peaceful, perhaps due in part to the sound of the water that echoed in people's minds and the negative ions produced by the falls. This has been scientifically proven to generate a feeling of well-being in human beings. It is with a certain sense of irony I note companies selling machines to replicate this environment in the homes of those who can afford it.

❧

Children had a wonderful time here. They would climb the rocks behind Celilo, walking above the chutes that bordered the edge of the river. You became everyone's child when you left your lodging. Relatives and villagers instructed, and occasionally scolded, the children. You had to behave. Every day was school for young children, learning by observance and eventual full participation in the day's activities and work. Individual contribution was the norm and each individual had respect regardless of ability. One could improve with practice. Young boys could fish at safer locations in the chutes to learn the skills they needed to move to the more dangerous places.

It had its risks. The rocks were wet and slippery. One photo from the period shows a boy being fished out of the falls. He had fallen into one of the chutes. Miraculously, he appeared in one of the fishers' dip nets. Pulled to safety on the platform, it was a lucky day for him.

This was a dangerous place and occasionally an unwatched child or unlucky fisher drowned.

An elder woman explained that if my generation knew the language, we would have no questions. We would hear these words directly from the teachings and songs. From time immemorial the Creator's instruction was direct and clear. Feasts and worship held in honor of the first roots and huckleberries are major events. The first salmon honored at Celilo had its head and tail placed back into *Nch'I-Wana*. The whole community honored the first catch: *One of our relatives has returned, and we consider the lives we take to care for our communities.*

Prayer may not be enough in this time and with the complexities we face to restore wild runs. We may see a vital piece of the circle absent. Absent like the old village and Celilo Falls.

It can be said that tribal peoples built the longhouses and Shaker churches for their spiritual comfort. It can also be said that great spiritual comfort is derived from the first salmon whose journey ends with a feast held in its honor. Together, tribal members and salmon weave a unique cultural fabric designed by the Divine Creator. What the mind cannot comprehend, the heart and spirit interpret. The result is a beautiful and

Elizabeth Woody

Miraculous rescue
of Danny Simpson
with a fishing net by
Archie Bushman and
an unidentified
man, 1952.

dignified ceremonial response to the Creator in appreciation for the willingness of Nature to serve humankind. These ceremonial homes and their leaders and participants have known each other since time immemorial. As natives to these lands, tribal members know the true freedom of religion. It manifests itself in PEACE, HAPPINESS, and STRENGTH.[1]

The songs in the "ceremonial response to the Creator" referred to above are phenomenal, repeated seven times by seven drummers, a bell ringer and people gathered in the Longhouse. *Washat* song is an ancient method of worship. Before the singing, dancers line up from eldest to the youngest in a circle around the rim of the open floor. Chief Thompson called this the open heart of Mother Earth.[2] By wearing the finest Indian dress they show respect to the Creator. Some have beaded and woven family heirlooms mixed with modern cloth ribbon shirts and bright wing dresses. Those who can, stand and rhythmically move their bodies with the bend of their knees. The swinging of their cupped hand to their heart signifies the gathering of the songs into their hearts. Some people bring large eagle feathers to swing.

They begin to move with men on the South side, women on the North.

In a pattern of a complete circle they dance sideways, counter-clockwise. Some dancers leap high. When they stop, they are North and South again. The drums in the West, the East is open towards the rising sun. The North holds the stationary seven drummers and the bell ringer. This ceremony illustrates the partnership of men and women, essential equality and the balance within the four directions and the cosmos. We each have our place and our role. As a result, the Longhouse is a special place to learn.

Meanwhile, in the kitchen, women cook the food for the meal. Salmon (*nusoox*), venison, the edible roots (*x'ash, sowītk, wak' amu, p'axī*) and the various berries—huckleberries and chokecherries—are the four sacred foods. Common types of food are added to the significant four on portable tables. Tule mats on the floor are traditional tables. The cooks have prepared the meal for long hours. Those who gather the roots and berries are distinguished. They are selected to gather the foods and, thus, recognized for their good hearts and minds. Tribal men who have hunted and fished are acknowledged for being fine persons. You do not gather food without proper training, so as to not disrupt the natural systems or "law of the land."

The prayer is led in song. With instruction in *Sahaptin*, the people take one of each sacred four to their plates with a cup of water beside them. In turn we pick up a sample of each and eat a small piece: the salmon, venison, roots and berries. Finally, the water is called for with a loud and long *"Chush!"* We drink and the ritual is finished.

My uncle explained to his children, "We travel from the river to the mountains with these foods." Even the order in which we taste the food travels from *Nch'I-Wana* to the white peaks of the volcanic Cascade range. Part of my ancestral geography, these mountains are presently called Adams and Hood.

The plenitude of these foods has drastically diminished. In 1995, having only 12,000 salmon passing the Bonneville Dam shocked Northwest communities, a drastic reduction from 2.5 million in 1993. There was a moratorium on ceremonial harvests in the Columbia River. This meant tribal leaders ordered designated fishermen to harvest only "Treaty-Sustainable" amounts of fish in tributaries where there were substantial runs. It was a frightening public acknowledgment of a species' endangerment.

The tribes sounded the alarm regarding exposure to waterborne toxins through contaminated fish, largely because native people on the Columbia

Elizabeth Woody

River consume fish at the average of 2.1 ounces a day, or nine times the national average. The EPA's survey revealed to the tribes: these toxins include dioxin, furans and other organochlorine chemicals in fish tissue. This is primarily from industrial polluters.[3]

My uncle, Lewis Pitt, said, "I like to eat those fish in peace, but today it's a scary proposition. The reality is we're not just talking of Indian people here. We're talking about all the citizens of Oregon and Washington. Today, the entire Columbia River in Oregon, all of the Snake River in Washington State and the Columbia River from Priest Rapids Dam to the Oregon-Washington border violate water quality criteria for dioxin (.013 parts per quadrillion)." Dioxin is a highly toxic chemical produced as a by-product of chlorine-using pulp and paper mills, from burning of waste by hospital and municipal incinerators, and from other polluters.[4] People were warned not to consume more than one fish a week if caught in the Columbia River.

Returning to my thoughts about the Longhouse and the Columbia River Plateau indigenous peoples' belief system, my younger relatives should feel pride in their history and lineage. It has not been such a long time from the era when we were free to practice and live by subsistence. It is hard to forget a time when people hated, feared and despised Indians. Once, as a child, a non-Indian neighbor girl came to visit and we watched an old western. The Indians rode over the rise, hooting and whooping. Her eyes got real big and she turned to look at my grandfather saying, "Ooo, Indians!" My grandfather said, "Honey, I'm an Indian." She emphatically shook her head, no. We weren't "Indians" to her.

In a sense we are not Indians. We have a specific name for ourselves and a location that we consider our place of origin. The effort to overpower and exploit the land has caused death to native people, animals, plants, water and soil. As the list of endangered species grows and species die, our global knowledge diminishes.

Removal of indigenous peoples of the last century is the precedent for the removal and expending of our natural resources, or as some now call it, our natural capital.* The Treaty of 1855 ceded 10.5 million acres of territory to the United States and retained certain inalienable rights. Tribes decide their membership and activities through an older sovereign government. These rights are retained through negotiation between sovereigns as pre-colonial, independent American nations. Our

*Natural capital: "The natural capital of a place is the productive capacity inherent in its healthy soil, clean water, native diversity and functioning natural systems." Ted Wolf of Ecotrust paraphrased this definition from the Shorebank and Ecotrust's Shorebank Pacific, The First Environmental Bancorporation's business plan.

claims come from a time before the existence of the United States. Living beings like salmon and foods are integral and significant in our lives, considerations we cannot ignore.

Salmon stocks found in the Columbia River may be as old as two to three million years. Many species are extinct today. While people can adapt to change faster than animals, it is the animals that die first. The damage requires a higher price tag the longer we wait.

Our religion, or cultural world, views science not as a field apart but as part of our law. The stories and native language contain our knowledge. Each generation acts with a responsibility for the next while examining the outcomes of the last. Maybe nature's intelligent laws have been breached, but not without consequence. Returning salmon are not as strong or as big as those in the past.

The core of my female self, the Great Mother, is joined to the land to provide nourishment through gathering. Another aspect of humanity, the male core, accesses this nourishment by a certain discipline in hunting and fishing. Centered on gathering and expressions of thankfulness, we learn well-defined gender roles within ceremonial life. We are bereft of honor in the separation from the river and the land. This adversely influences our partnership with other living beings. Descendants, like myself, do not learn the language or how to live if this modern world collapsed. Most of the world lives without the electricity we take for granted. The lessons innate in my culture include the history of specific relationships established in a culture that codifies and bonds animals and people.

Celilo Falls illustrates the story of inadequacy and ignorance of this land. The story begins even before that event with the building of ambitions to make an Eden where Eden was not needed. One only needs to learn from the land how to live upon it.

In history, another form of story, we can scrutinize the primary causes for the loss of salmon and habitat. The mainstream *Nch'I-Wana* is broken up by nineteen mega hydro-electric dams, many built without plans for the cyclic route of the salmon. Nuclear, agricultural and industrial pollution, the evaporation of water from broad surfaces of reservoirs and destructive clear-cuts are detrimental to salmon. Since 1855, the *Nch'I-Wana*'s 14 million salmon and steelhead have dwindled to 2.5 million in 1991, 150,000 in 1995 and just 75,000 in 1996.

The 1994 endangered list noted three species of salmon. The massive cutting of evergreen forests has changed our

Elizabeth Woody

land's ability to produce what it once had. Felled trees crash down at a rate faster than those in tropical rain forests.

While hard cash matters and loss-of-job issues are the new cant for those who protest conservation, there is no one who is singularly responsible. Corporations move on to cheaper resources all over the world when the old disappears. Reported submersion of whole trees in cold bays to save their value in rarity is one example of predicted obsolescence. Our present economy has no provision, no *right*, for citizens to have jobs. We cannot regenerate biologically diverse forests in our lifetime because this takes centuries. What tribes I have mentioned have signed a valid document called a treaty. It has been said to hold an inalienable right to honor and protect their heritage and the ancient ecosystem on which this heritage relies. Tribal leaders often negotiate with policy makers for the benefit of many.

The practice of traditional awareness in a simple, direct way is to take only what we need, and let the rest grow. How does one know what is traditional? How can one learn? My uncle reminded me that we learned about simplicity first. He said, "The stories your grandmother told. Remember when she said her great-grandmother, *Kah-Nee-Ta*, would tell her to go to the river and catch some fish for the day. Your grandmother would catch several fish, because she loved looking at them. She would let all but two go. Her grandmother taught her that." A larger sorrow shadows my maternal grandparent's story of childhood loss of the material and intangible. What if the wild salmon no longer return? I cannot say if we have the necessary strength to face this impending loss.

While we may feel an impotent opposition to systemic greed, we are not without power. We need a dream of the future and to find the ability to realize this vision by practice of native applications to find meaning. Some find a need to live for their children, as my grandparents believed. These are the characteristics that enable survival. People who respect the Columbia River as a system may possess the vision for the survival of the salmon. An individual provocation from here informed by noble intent and study can make a difference. Our mission, ethics, entity and collaborative spirit must include a contract between individuals and a "Higher Power" as I have observed in ceremonial life. As a creative unit, and out of necessity, we must construct a learning society throughout, teaching the art of making connections, all of which is fundamental to the system's thinking. Differences are an asset in collective wisdom. "You think because you understand *one*, you must understand *two* and that one and one makes two, but you must also understand *and*" (Sufi Teaching). Saving salmon is an effort to save ourselves.

Arthur Dye, the director of Ecotrust, says, "All of us have the capacity and personal influence we are not using. The challenge is to find the resources not used within ourselves and figure out how to use them wisely. Even in dark times, people have a right to expect some ray of hope from their leaders. Often this is small scale because this may be all the influence we have." Ecotrust Board member Connie Best once said, "Even a small object can cast a large shadow if it is held up to light." In a human scale we are all potential leaders and true leaders must teach.

Giving in and being an American is a tough road to travel, because being one in many ways is devoid of responsibility when we do not make decisions or accept responsibility. The fallacy is that we are individual and alone. Decision requires feeling and caring. Creativity dies without heart. Our pack instincts and frustrations call on the "other" to blame.

We are past discovery and colonization. Integration of our universal values must include those who cannot speak. The salmon, the tree and even Celilo Falls (*Wyam*) echo within if we become still and listen. Once heard and understood, take only what you need and let the rest grow.

Sources cited:

1. Columbia River Inter-Tribal Fish Commission. *Annual Report.* Portland, OR, 1994, p. 15.

2. McKeown, Martha Ferguson. *Welcome to Our Salmon Feast.* Binfords & Mort, 1959 Portland, OR, p. 32.

3. *Wana Chinook Tymoo.* Issue 1, 1995 Portland, OR, pp. 4–5.

4. Ibid.

Note:
All native words are spelled phonetically.

Elizabeth Woody

Conversion

Changeable surface, sand, wind, brushes of grass.
The composition of small particles and abalone shell
a mutable language, fluid and clean,
tonal lilting in attenuated motion.

On the surface, removed from image,
an iridescent garment of compassion.
Boulders are lapped in flow,
voices ascend to the lunar disk.
Simple paintbrush bloom, ecstatic, in orange and red.

Salmon pass through the river's mouth,
Songs hum in the vocal throat of grace.

Sagebrush around the loving fire waits
in aureole of pale courage. Hold still,
touch the compact smoldering soil.
The flesh of salmon is translucent as flame.
Heat and ardor, tender interior, smoke and calm weeds.
The fire is a furious matter of watching.

Familiar warm air rises as the red tailed hawk, slow and loose,
a pinpoint of vision on movement.
Land uplifts the shadow, higher.
Sun raises the cottonwood branches from the river's surface.

The salmon wait inside rippling light on reversal of current.
The song says, Come or pass. Be weak or strong. Dance on light.

Moon is in the color of pale bellies' slow turn to sky.
Scales illumine desire. Loosened moon particles collect
on the fringe of grass and water.

A brittle sheen of calcium and light combine with radiance.
Fine combs of supple and rigid spines rest
among the stone.
The root, stone, flesh
and water.

Eʟɪᴢᴀʙᴇᴛʜ Wᴏᴏᴅy (Navajo/ Warm Springs/Wasco/Yakama) is a visual artist as well as a writer. She has published poetry, short fiction and essays. She says her grandmother used to tell her, "If you can make something, you can never be poor." Taking that advice to heart, she is a fervent "maker," a term of praise for *poet* that poets use for one another.

Her first collection of poetry, *Hand Into Stone*, received the American Book Award. Her second and third collections of writing were published in 1994, *Luminaries of the Humble* and *Seven Hands, Seven Hearts: Prose and Poetry*. She received the William Stafford Memorial Award for Poetry from the Pacific Northwest Booksellers' Association in 1995, the Americans for Indian Opportunity Ambassadors 1993 Fellowship and a Brandywine Visiting Artist Fellowship in 1986.

Ms. Woody has been a professor of creative writing at the Institute of American Indian Arts in Santa Fe. She presently works as a Program Associate at the non-profit environmental organization, Ecotrust of Portland, Oregon.

Elizabeth Woody

NADYEZHDA DUVAN

The Ulchi World View

*As told to and
translated by
Jan Van Ysslestyne*

The Ulchis are the descendants of the Tungus tribes of Ilou, Mohe and Pohai, a southern speaking Manchu-Tungus language group. The northern section of the Amur River region of Siberia is their home. In the nineteenth century they numbered around 1,500 people but have now grown to 2,500 according to the most recent census counts taken in the early 1980s.

The spiritual life of the Ulchi is based on an animistic world view. Animism is the belief that spirits inhabit the world and have an effect on the lives of people, animals and objects. The Ulchis, both past and present, conceive of everything in existence as living beings endowed with reason, spirit and power. Mountains, rivers, lakes, oceans, rocks and forests all have their own spirit masters. The Gods and Goddesses are the Siberian Tiger, the Bear, the Dragon of the Cosmos and the Sun and Moon.

According to the Ulchi's conception of the universe, the world is divided into three distinct parts. The Upperworld is called Ba and is ruled by Enduri, the Dragon King of the Cosmos. The Ulchis say that there are seven layers to this world. Among the inhabitants are the star peoples, ancestors, deceased shamans, and the Ebaha—beautiful vampiric female spirits who are known to attack and kill living people. All types of birds are considered to be spirits of the heavens.

The Middleworld, known as the Taiga, is the land of mortal people. The Siberian Tiger, called Amba and the Bear, known as Mapaw (Grandfather) are the deities to this region. It is here that the land spirits, water spirits and Mountain Goddess reign supreme. The daily lives and rituals of the Ulchi center around these Middleworld spirits.

The Underworld is called the land of Buni. This is the world in which the souls of the dead travel to begin their next life. When a member of the community dies, a special type of funeral rite is held for a period of one year, the time it takes for the soul to walk the road to the land of Buni. There, he or she will live in a new village, meet with old friends, and continue with all of the daily activities of hunting and fishing.

These three worlds are located parallel to each other and exist outside of time and space. The geography is the same; there are animals, mountains, forests, rivers and oceans in all of the worlds. The Ulchi image of this three-world-unity is their Tree of Life. The upper branches of the Tree represent the Cosmos; the center section, or trunk, is the Taiga; and the lower section and roots symbolize the world of Buni.

Temu—The God of the Waters and the Ritual to the Salmon

Traditionally, our primary source of food was the salmon, which traveled up the Amur from the Sea of Okhotsk. Twice a year, in the spring and fall, a special ceremony is still held to insure the arrival of salmon. Ulchis believe that of all of the natural elements, water is the most powerful and dangerous. The God of the rivers, oceans and lakes is called Temu. He is seen as an old grandfather who lives in his underwater kingdom. In common with the belief that all of the three worlds have the same topography, this underwater kingdom has villages, people and is inhabited by the creatures of the sea.

Nedyezhda traveling the Amur River on her way to the islands for a mushroom gathering expedition.

The water ritual addresses this ancient grandfather in the hope that he will send the fish to the nets of the fishermen. If the ritual is performed properly the spirit of the water will appear. He is an ancient man who knows and sees all. That is why we must be very, very, very cautious when addressing water spirits. We must never defile their sacred places, never speak harshly of them and never laugh or speak too loudly around water.

The ritual begins with the carving of the sacred sticks. These sticks must be made of willow that grows from the riverbank. Food offerings of tobacco, berries, salmon, rice or millet and the sacred grass, called *wacee*, are placed in a little white boat made of birch bark. The sacred sticks are stuck into the water, close to the riverbank, about twelve inches apart, and the little boat of food offerings is sailed out into the river between these two sticks. Prayers are then said from the heart to Temu. We don't ask the spirits to send the big fish. We will always say, "Send us the tiny fish, whatever you can send. Send us the little fish." A person should never take more from the world than he or she needs. Fishermen would only take from the river what they needed to feed their own family.

After the prayers are given and the

Nedyezhda Duvan's father, Dumben, with his two wives and eight of their twenty-five children, circa 1930.

having observed this style of dress, called the Ulchis *yup'itatzi*, "fish skin Tartars."

Currently, in my village of Bulava, only a few masters still know how to prepare and create our fish skin garments. These masters are elderly grandmothers, commissioned primarily by museums to make the traditional clothing that represents the indigenous folk arts of the people of the Russian Far East.

boat has been launched, we wait and watch to see how quickly the ritual boat is taken by the water. The speed with which the boat is taken from the bank and the boat's relation to the sticks reveals how the offering is received by the spirit powers of the water.

Ulchis use every part of the fish. We use the kidneys, the liver, the bones, the skin and the bladder, which is the primary source of natural glue know as *darpu*. Everything has a place and everything a purpose. Everything has meaning. The vertebrae and the cheekbones are dried to make rattles that hang over children's cradles. Everyone knows this is what keeps us safe from unwanted spirits. We also use the skin to make dresses, hats, boots, pants and jackets that keep us dry when we are out in our boats in the rain. The ancient Chinese,

Ulchi Clan Creation Myths

The creation of the clan names of the Ulchi peoples is founded upon myths and legends of where and how each family came into existence. The Ulchis speak of a time, long ago, when a beautiful maiden married a great Siberian Tiger. It was from this union that the Ulchis came into this world. Each family tells a different story of their beginnings. Some families say that they came from the mating of a female human with a tree or animal spirit. Others say that their clan is associated with a particular land spirit, as in the name of Duvan, which means the top of a spirit mountain that overlooks the village of Bulava. The story of the Anga clan traces its beginnings back to an age very long ago. This story was told by the great shaman, Tika Anga. A seventh-generation shaman born in 1911, she

Nadyezhda Duvan

resided in the village of Bulava until her death in 1998. She was the most powerful shaman in the Ulchi tribe, known as a Kasa shaman, the highest ranking shaman of her people. Her spirit husband was a Siberian Tiger and together they produced two tiger cubs who have grown to be her major spirit helpers. The word shaman originally comes from the Ulchi language.

The Anga Clan Legend

A very long time ago, there lived a young woman on the banks of the Amur River. She was an only child when tragedy struck her life. Her parents died

Grandmother
Tiki Anga.

suddenly, leaving her alone to fend for herself.

One day a great rain storm came up from the river. She looked out to the Amur and saw a great large fish head rising up from under the waves. First she saw a head and then a tail. The storm grew stronger and stronger as she watched the fish moving toward the shore. The fish came out of the water and began to roll uphill toward her home.

The young woman thought to herself, "This must be the master of the river!" The great fish rolled up to the threshold of the home and spoke to her in a human voice. "Cook me quickly, eat me and go to sleep!" This young girl, too frightened to disobey the river master, did what was instructed of her. She cooked and ate this fish and fell fast asleep.

Later, she woke up in the middle of the night. The house was almost completely dark. A small fire was burning in the hearth. The girl thought she had an unusual dream. As she looked around her home, there, standing in the corner, was a great large fish. She watched the fish transform into a handsome young man.

He entered her bed and they became as man and wife. The couple lived together and gave birth to three sons.

Grandfather Misha Duvan, one of Nedyezhda's great teachers and the last male shaman of the Ulchis at a Geeva performance.

The family was happy but the children were sometimes lonely. Within a few years, the family decided to move across the river in order to be closer to other people. The children began to play with other youngsters and grew into strong and handsome men. "You see," says Grandmother Tika, "our family comes from the fish."

Nadyezhda shares with us this traditional story of the Salmon Spirit.

The Salmon Spirit

A very, very long time ago along the Amur River lived an old woman and an old man. They were childless but lived with a cat and a dog. The cat and the dog were having a great long talk at home.

"Oh, it isn't good in winter time," said the dog. "Food is very scarce in the *taiga* and I'm hungry."

Nadyezhda Duvan

The village of Bulava on the Amur River.

"I wish I could have some fish," said the cat, "but the master said that the fish went somewhere far away from the bank of the river."

A little time later the old man came out of his home and decided to try to find some fish. He was a good man who observed all the laws of the *taiga*, but sometimes it seemed that his luck had disappeared. In the evening he came back to his home in very low spirits and told his wife, "I have caught only one small salmon. Take it and make some soup, and don't forget about the cat and the dog."

The old woman brought extra wood to the stove and began to kindle the fire. She drew out a very sharp knife to cut the salmon into pieces. All of a sudden the salmon spoke to her in a human voice, "Oh, Mother of the house! Scrape off my scales and make your soup with them but let me go back to the river. I have hundreds of children who cannot live without me."

The old woman was shocked. Never before had she had a talk with any fish. She felt great pity for the small youngsters and decided to let their mother return to the river.

Later on, when the water in the pot began to boil, she put in some of the scales that she had gathered from the fish. She added some herbs and salt and sat down to see what would happen. Soon the home was filled with a wonderful smell.

The old man soon returned to the home and as he entered, smelling the air, he said, "You can always tell a salmon from any other fish. There is only one small fish but it smells like a pot of fish."

The old woman told him the story about the salmon and her appeal for mercy. The old woman was afraid to look inside the pot. She said, "I do not know what could possibly be inside, but the smell is making me so very hungry."

"Why should you fear looking inside?" said the old man. "Have you done any wrong? You have acted with kindness and mercy, which are the laws of the *taiga*. Hey! Let me do it." The old man took off the lid of the pot and looked inside. Then he sat down and began crying. "You told me, old woman, that you had only put in the scales, but now the pot is full of salmon." The old woman and old man and the cat and the dog sat down and ate the greatest dinner that they could remember.

Since that time the old man was always lucky in his fishing and his wife cooked well. Nobody was ever hungry in that home again.

(Translated from Ulchi.)

Nadyezhda Duvan

98

Nedyezhda Duvan
at sixteen.

born to the Duvan family. Due to disease and injury, only five children survived into adulthood.

During the late 1960s, Nadyezhda was one of only two indigenous people to be given a scholarship to the newly formed Soviet Academy of Arts and Dance, founded in the city of Khabarovsk. She received her degree in choreography and decided to return to her village. She traveled to several Siberian communities to study with other notable indigenous dance masters. Preservation of these ancient dance movements became her passion. She continued studying and performing until 1984 when she became director of the Ulchi Folk Ensemble, *Geeva*. Today, as a paid artist for the Russian Federation (formally the Soviet State), she continues her directorship of *Geeva* as well as the children's ensemble, *Geero*. Both groups have traveled to countries in Western Europe: Germany, France, Italy and Switzerland, as well as Eastern European countries.

As Wisdom Keeper of the Ulchis, Nadyezhda records the stories and legends of her people. She meets with the remaining elders to document the rich oral traditions of the Ulchi people. Her husband, Kola, is a master carver and her two daughters, Vita and Kshusa, are members of the *Geeva* ensemble.

NADYEZHDA DUVAN (Ulchi) was born in 1950 in the village of Bulava, Ulchi region, territory of Khabarovsk. Her father, Dumbin, born in 1885, was a great hunter and leader of his clan. He had two wives, which was traditional until very recent times. Goga, born in 1898, his second wife, was Nadyezhda's mother. Between these two wives, twenty-five children were

Nedyezhda Duvan
and Jan Van Ysslestyne
at Seattle's SeaTac
Airport, 1992.

JAN VAN YSSLESTYNE
has studied the traditions of the Ulchi
people since 1992. She is one of only a
handful of people outside of the culture
who speaks and translates the Ulchi
language. She is the assistant director
of Amba, created in 1993 by Nadyezhda
Duvan. It is the only school of Siberian
Shamanism in the world. The purpose
of the school is to teach the rich oral
traditions, dances, philosophy and
manual folk arts to the people of the
West.

Because there is neither phone nor
fax in Nadyezhda's village of Bulava,
and travel is extremely difficult in winter, when preparing this manuscript, Jan
went far out of her way to communicate
with Nadyezhda to get her contribution.
The two talked by appointment on
radio and arranged to have the pieces
hand-carried from Siberia to Seattle to
be translated in the nick of time for
inclusion in the book.

Nadyezhda Duvan

NORA MARKS DAUENHAUER

Five Slices of Salmon

1. Introduction

The first European and Euro-American explorers to Southeast Alaska found us Tlingits in various places drying salmon. We Tlingits have always been eating salmon.

There are five species of salmon in Alaska: king, or Chinook, which is the largest; sockeye, or red; coho, or silver; chum, or dog salmon; and humpy (hump-back), or pink. Salmon eggs hatch in fresh water; salmon spend most of their developing years in salt water, and return to their home stream during the summer months to spawn and die. During this phase, their color and shape change dramatically.

Not only have we always used salmon as our main diet, and not only has it been the mainstay of our subsistence and commercial economies, but the different varieties of salmon are a part of our social structure and ethnic identity as well. Beyond the physical use of salmon as food, salmon have symbolic and totemic value. Many clans have salmon as their crest. My clan is called *Lukaax̲.ádi* in Tlingit; the name derives from a salmon river in Duncan Canal near Petersburg, Alaska. Our principal emblem is the sockeye or red salmon.

The *L'uknax̲.ádi* clan derives its Tlingit name from another place of origin, related to the Tlingit word for coho salmon, which is their principal crest. The *L'eineidí* clan has the dog salmon as its crest and the *Kwaashk'ikwaan* use the humpy or hump-back salmon. Increasingly most Tlingit clans are becoming known by the English names of their principal crest animal; thus the above-mentioned groups are commonly called Sockeye Clan, Coho Clan, Dog Salmon Clan, etc.

Tlingit clans historically owned areas of economic production that were most often also places of importance in the Tlingit spiritual geography. Many of these places are important salmon rivers. For example, my clan, the *Lukaax̱.ádi* (sockeye) owned part of the Alsek River and we have among our clan crests *Heen Kwéiyi*, known in English as Gateway Knob, where the salmon migrate up the Alsek River. Our clan also traditionally owned Chilkoot Lake and Chilkoot River, near Haines.

This enduring relationship between the Tlingit people, the fish and animals, the land and the connection of all of these to our social structure took many generations to evolve. The personal experiences of ancestors with the various forms of life and landscape are passed down in the oral tradition and visual art of each clan. In this way the education of the future stewards of a clan crest or tribal lands traditionally took place, informing the upcoming generation how to handle crests properly, when to handle them, who should handle them and how to talk about them. Tradition-

ally minded Tlingit people wear and otherwise display their clan crests during ceremonies such as memorials for the departed. The crest designs alluding to the events are inscribed or painted on, carved, sewn or woven as ceremonial objects. Our crest art objects function as our ancestors, identifying us as being their descendants. This is the way I was raised, as we moved from place to place in a very conservative, Tlingit-speaking extended family, following the subsistence lifestyle.

Images of salmon are important throughout Tlingit and other Alaska Native oral tradition. In her telling of "The Glacier Bay History," the late Susie James focused on the salmon run as a central image of the "myth of eternal return," that when people live in harmony with the cosmos, the salmon return in abundance and the land provides. In another story, probably very ancient, and popular in Tsimshian and Haida oral literature as well as Tlingit (and claimed by all of them as a clan crest), a young boy rejects the dryfish his mother offers him because part of it is moldy. This offends the salmon people, and as part of the child's education, he is "captured" by the salmon people. He eventually returns home with the salmon run, is recognized by his people (because the necklace he always wore was now around a salmon neck), is restored to human form and becomes a shaman and cultural mediator between humans and the salmon. The *Koyukon Athabaskan* people of Interior Alaska have a wonderful riddle: *We come upstream in red canoes.* The answer, of course, is salmon.

The crest objects may be also considered deeds to land in traditional use and ownership by the group using the crest. In a striking example of this, our late clan leader from Haines wore his Chilkat robe with the sockeye salmon design as evidence in a court dispute over our clan's ownership of the land on which our clan house is situated. "We wear our history," he testified.

With the arrival of Euro-Americans many Tlingit and other Alaska native people were separated from their land and resource base. For example, many canneries were built at the mouth of salmon streams traditionally claimed by Tlingit clans and used for subsistence fishing. Tlingit people historically practiced subsistence hunting, fishing and logging without dominating or destroying the natural resource. Traditional Tlingit fish traps were woven and could be hand carried. In contrast, the canneries built barge-size fish traps that were anchored along the migration routes, intercepting thousands of salmon on their way to spawn. Entire salmon runs

were depleted by fish traps and by logging practices that ruined habitat. The Tlingit protested fish traps and the usurping of their land, but to little avail. In 1953 President Eisenhower declared the fishing communities of Southeast Alaska a disaster area. Fish traps were outlawed only in 1959, with the coming of Alaska statehood. The controversy over subsistence continues to rage.

As with land, subsistence is at the very core of our ethnic identity and tribal existence. The importance of salmon goes beyond the question of calories. It is part of our identity. We need salmon to continue as physically, mentally and spiritually healthy people.

The period described in my two childhood pieces is of the mid-1930s to the early 1940s. Although my father eagerly embraced new technology, his values and those of the extended family were very conservative. He was the first to get a gas or diesel engine, but we were among the last families who still followed a traditional subsistence lifestyle, and who still spoke only Tlingit at home. I was eight years old before I started school and first heard English. This time was still before freezers. We preserved salmon in dryfish camp the way Tlingits had been doing it forever. Our family lived on a boat. Before World War II we wintered in

Nora Marks Dauenhauer

Purse seiner in southeast Alaska in the 1970s. The line drawn through the pulley closes the seine net into a purse.

tents at Graves Harbor and other sites on the outer Pacific Coast of what is now Glacier Bay National Park. It was a moving experience to revisit the sites of my childhood with a park service archeologist in 1997 and find the remains of tentsites and workshops of more than fifty years ago. The war and truant officers gradually brought this era to a close, but the memories remain.

Having first looked at salmon in a more conceptual adult, academic and anthropological way, I now invite you to share in four more slices of salmon from different points of view: childhood memories of trolling for king salmon; memories of our traditional dryfish camp; a modern play based on an old and outrageous story; and a nostalgic urban poem.

2. Trolling

I woke to something hitting the deck outside. It sounded like a salmon slamming its tail on the deck. Before long there was another of the same noise, then another and another. Wow! My father must be filling up the fish bin by his girdies, and the salmon are still bouncing.

I wanted to see what was happening, so I quickly jumped out of my bunk and dressed. On my rush through the galley I grabbed a piece of bread for breakfast and started up the stairs to the back deck. I could see that it was a clear day, with a lot of sky.

When my father came into view, he was busy. He looked like he was tangled in a bundle of steel, and at the same time he looked like he was juggling salmon. Fish were flipping everywhere. The sounds were incredible: the flipping wires, the musical sound of the spoons, the gaff slamming salmon. He had in his right hand a gaff hook that doubled as a club for the salmon. He was hooking the salmon with his right hand as he pulled his power girdie on with his left. The deck was alive with flipping salmon. My father was trying to keep them from sliding overboard. All the while he was looking for which of the four trolling poles should be pulled up next.

They were king salmon! Of all salmon, the most beautiful is the king, which is also called Chinook. When freshly caught it's very light-silvery and dark silver, with iridescent pink and blue in the scales and black dots along the back and side. The head is mostly black inside the mouth. When they're caught and flipping, they flash like a pouring out of multi-colored jewels. They curl every which way. They twist in crescent shapes like silver bracelets inlaid or studded with jewels.

After he had let the line back down again, with its hooks and shining spoons, he yelled, "Nora! Get a knife and start cleaning the salmon! Get the ones that aren't flipping!"

"What fun!" I thought. I ran downstairs, found a sharp knife and ran back on deck. I started cleaning as fast as I could.

My father said, "Let me see. Gills

Patrick Venner, Nora's grandson, overwhelmed by his catch. Douglas, Alaska, early 1990s.

first, then the belly. Take your time, but do a good job. Clean them good. Remember, the fish buyers check how they look inside."

As he said this, my two brothers, Alex and Raymond, came on deck still yawning from a heavy sleep. Pop said, "You guys start cleaning the salmon with your sister. One of you wash them and cover them with a gunny sack. Put the clean salmon in the salmon box. Lay them out so that we can put a lot in. Wash the box with fresh water!" He meant sea water. The gulls were going crazy in anticipation.

We continued like this for a while, then the frenzy started slowing down. My father was smiling the whole day. We didn't stop, even after the biting frenzy slowed to almost nothing.

While the salmon were really biting, Mom poked her head out from time to time. She was at the wheel all during the good fishing. She circled back each time she thought she had passed the school of salmon.

Only after Pop sold the salmon did we kids find out that what we had experienced that day was once-in-a-lifetime luck. My father was at the right time at the right place, and came on a migrating school of salmon. It was great for all of us who experienced it. We were very happy.

Nora Marks Dauenhauer

All the time we were busy we were wishing for Grandma Eliza and Aunty Anny, whom we had left at our home port to look for natural foods from the forest and beaches, so they didn't witness the fishing frenzy.

It was my first experience as a salmon cleaner. I have never seen another school of salmon bite like that before or since.

3. Dryfish Camp

Pop had anchored the *New Anny* by the coho salmon stream where we traveled every year to gather our winter supply of fish for the entire extended family. It was at the head of a deep inlet off of Icy Strait, not too far from Glacier Bay. Everyone was excited and talking all at once.

"*Nás'k handid áwé yángaa kugeix,*" someone was saying, "Three hundred is usually enough."

Pop was cooking, usually salmon and its various parts, possibly the head. Aunty Anny was saying, "I'll help gather the salmon."

Pop said, "I wish she would stay on board, and not come along. We really don't have much room on the sealing boat. It's tippy." He more or less mumbled it, so Aunty didn't hear him. She was all ready to go.

Grandma Eliza always managed to convince her sons (Jim, John, and Willie) to get at least three hundred salmon for drying in the fall of every year. Over the years her sons had built four smokehouses in three different places for her and the family. An older, and now a newer one, were near the entrance of the inlet where we were anchored. The third smokehouse was at another protected cove nearby and was used for drying halibut in spring. At the start of World War II, when travel to the Pacific Ocean end of Icy Strait was restricted, they built the fourth smoke- house at another natural harbor at the inland end of Icy Strait. This became our last stop before winter. But that's another story.

We, the children on board *New Anny*, were keeping our eyes on the river where our father and uncles had gone to get salmon. We no sooner looked, when we would be looking again. Then what looked like a drift log floated out of the mouth of the river. Another followed, then a third.

As they got closer, the logs looked as if their branches were tipping ever so slightly. We thought the branches dipped like oars. Then we saw they were oars that looked like branches. It moved so slowly. It was one of the sealing boats they had filled almost to the brim with salmon. They were so low in the water that at first they looked like logs. They were rowing so slowly so the salmon wouldn't shift in the boat and tip it over. When they were closer out in the bay, you could almost see the shapes of the people in the boats.

We watched them coming all the way to the side of *New Anny*. When they got near to us, we could see they had a lot of salmon. We kids were happy. My little brothers were jumping for joy. The salmon were all water-marked with red—mostly cohos and chums. The chums were green with some red and black circles on their bodies. According to tradition they are the claw marks of a brown bear. All of the salmon heads were gray and black—they were beautiful. We could see all the salmon in the rowboats as they got next to our bigger boat.

My father said, "Start boiling water for boiled salmon!" One of the boys ran down to the galley to start the boiling water. My father had his favorite treat already soaking in cold water—the finest coho heads and tails, to be eaten raw.

We children watched as they unloaded their catch. The other boats rowed up to *New Anny*. They had a lot of salmon, but not quite enough. They had to go back and get more.

When I was older, I got to share in

what happened on shore. We always went to get our salmon for smoking from there. My father set the net by going upriver from us with my brother Alex in a rowboat. As they started off, my brother threw the seine overboard while my father yelled "Let 'er go!" and rowed, smiling, toward the opposite shore. Almost crossing the river, he turned toward us on the beach downstream from where he started out.

When he was close and Alex was laughing and almost out of net, we waited to catch him on the shore. When he hit the beach, we grabbed the bow line and someone grabbed the end of the lead line and the cork line of the net, and we started pulling in the net. The corks on the net were dancing on the river. We knew this meant there were salmon in there.

While we were pulling up the net—my brothers Alex and Raymond, my father, Willie, and our deck hand Eddy Jackson—we could begin to see the salmon in the net. Some of the cohoes were red; others were still silver. The chum or dog salmon were green, black, and red. Some of us were shouting and having a great time.

We worked fast. You have to when you do this kind of work. So as the net pulled the salmon on the beach, we grabbed them and threw them up where

Nora Marks Dauenhauer

108

smoke and dry the salmon. We'd stay there a month or so—as long as it took to prepare the food for winter.

❧

When we got to dryfish camp it was almost night. We could hear an owl hooting in the woods.

The next day was preparation for butchering salmon. The men lined up two sealing boats on the beach during the morning high tide and filled them half up with sea water.

After sharpening their knives, they were ready. They butchered by cutting the head off and gutting them. We split the salmon down along one side of the backbone, cutting through the small, rib-like bones, but not through the skin. One side of the split salmon has the tail, which is then broken, not cut away.

Every one of the adults was butchering salmon and putting them in the boats full of salt water. Once in a while they stirred the water. Anyone who wasn't butchering was carrying a salmon or two in each hand to go into the smokehouse where they were hung, flesh side in, over sticks that reached from wall to wall.

Some of the men made tables out of boards or good-sized boxes. Grandma sat at the edge of the beach rye grass.

they wouldn't flutter into the river again and swim away. The entire bank of the river was aflutter with silver, red, green and red. The band where the seine was was like a giant necklace of diamonds, rubies, emeralds and rubies. It was a sight to see.

My Aunty Anny had a club in her hand to hit the salmon on the nose. This is how we caught our salmon in the river. We set our net over and over until we had enough fish for the winter.

When we had enough fish on board, Pop would weigh anchor, and the family would move with the catch to the smokehouse site, where we would

Nora holding up a fillet of salmon to be dried. Juneau, mid 1980s.

She had toppled some over and was using the bunches as a pad to cut her salmon on. This was her layer of protection against sand and gravel. She didn't need very much equipment—just her knife and gloves. Grandma always moved slowly, but she was steady and she never quit!

As they butchered they saved the heads, especially the large ones. They split these. At low tide the men dug a large pit and lined it with skunk cabbage. Then they put a bunch of innards from the salmon in it. On top of this they put the salmon heads. They kept on adding the innards and layering the heads, spread open. This is how we make k'ínk'—fermented fish heads. There are four tides a day: two high and two low. The rising and falling tide rinses and flushes the fish heads with natural brine. In about two weeks they are ready to eat. In this way, we filled the smokehouse with fish and the pit on the beach with salmon heads.

While we smoked the salmon, our father trolled for king salmon. When he trolled and the weather was too bad for fish buyers to come by, or if it was too far for him to go in the bad weather, he salted the salmon in kegs for winter use.

Some of the women went berry picking while we smoked the salmon. After three or four days of smoking salmon and picking berries, the entire family began splitting the hanging salmon for the second phase of drying, being careful not to mash or split the flesh. The men hand the fish down from the drying racks to the women, who are splitting the salmon. The women carefully slice them and fillet for strips. This is one of the tastiest parts of dried salmon, called in Tlingit *at yuwaa x̲'éeshi*.

For lunch or dinner we cooked half-smoked fish tails either on barbeque sticks or boiled. When done, you can dip them into seal oil. Tasty! This is very delicious after berry picking, especially with fresh berries for dessert. The berries included blueberries, huckleberries, lowbush cranberries and elderberries. Elderberries must be cooked. Some of the time we got fresh fruit, such as watermelon or canteloupe from the fish buyers, but not too much. Sometimes

Nora Marks Dauenhauer

Nora Marks Dauenhauer admires the smokehouse artistry of Haida "Auggie" Anderson near Sitka, Alaska, early 1970s.

we had salmon eggs with seaweed for lunch or dinner.

When the salmon were coated with smoke after being sliced, we often had some for dinner, especially those that were cracked or mashed by accident. The half-dried salmon is called *náayadi* in Tlingit. We also had fresh king salmon that Papa caught on his power boat.

We stayed almost a month smoking the salmon. Approximately a week before they are completely dry, all of the salmon are skewered on sticks that hold them up by their side bones. They are raised to a higher level of the smokehouse. At this time we use larger fires but we have to be careful not to make the fire too big. The family still talks about how Uncle Jimmy once put so much wood on the smokehouse fire that he nearly burned the smokehouse down. But that's another story.

When all the salmon were smoked we packed up, broke camp and headed to Hoonah or Juneau for the winter. The three hundred-plus salmon were going to be our main diet all winter. The dryfish was divided four ways: Grandma, Grandpa and Aunty Anny; our family— Willie and Emma Marks and us kids; Uncle Jim, Aunty Jenny and our cousin, Horace; Uncle John, Aunty Mary and their daughter Elizabeth. For each fam-

ily this amounted to about seventy-five salmon, plus the byproducts such as strips from the second splitting, salmon tails that will be used until gone and salmon eggs—some in berry pudding already and some fermenting in kegs. The fermented heads were all eaten up directly from the pit, where the daily cycle of high and low tides washed and rinsed them.

Another delicacy we put up at the end of dryfish camp was fermented salmon eggs packed in seal stomachs along with dried salmon strips. The eggs are mashed and pounded and pushed into the stomach and the dried strips are also pushed in. Whenever seals were shot and butchered, the stomachs were inflated and dried and set aside for when it was time to use them. This was a kind of Tlingit "power bar" of my childhood, and I often get nostalgic for them.

My fondest memories of dryfish camp are of the site at the eastern end of Icy Strait. The site was selected for its multiple uses. Not only was it near the source of fish from streams or trolling, but berries were abundant and the hunting was good. We could leave for our winter village not only with dryfish and salt-fish and fermented fish-eggs, but also with deer meat and berries. The berries! Sometimes Pop would get angry with the women, grumbling, "Too many berries!" as he tried to find a place to put them on the boat, but in the winter they tasted so good as dessert after eating the salmon dryfish!

4. Raven, King Salmon and the Birds

A play based on Raven Stories *by Katherine Mills and George Davis, written for Naa Kahidi Theater, first performed in 1989 in Alaska, Washington and Oregon.*

CHARACTERS:
Storyteller (the only speaking role, except for "chorus" phrase said by the entire cast)

DANCERS WEARING MASK AND WING COSTUMES:
Raven
Robin
Chickadee
Steller's Jay
Magpie

PROPS:
Plastic club or long balloon
Stump
Greenstone
Skunk cabbage leaves
Salmon (may be either a prop or dancer)

MUSIC:
Raven Song, "Du Yaa Kanagoodi"

CULTURAL NOTES:
Skunk cabbage (Lysichitum americanum): *These grow exceptionally tall in the rainforest of Southeast Alaska, sometimes overhead. The leaves are used for wrapping and cooking.*

Ei, haaw!
An expression called out by Tlingit fishermen of Southeast Alaska when they spot a salmon jumping.

Nora Marks Dauenhauer

ANB *(Alaska Native Brotherhood):*
A social and political organization founded
in 1912, important advocate for Native civil
rights and land claims legislation.

Scene 1
Beach in Southeast Alaska

Storyteller:
Raven, walking along a beach.
He sees King Salmon
jumping out of the water.

Chorus: (as Salmon jumps)
Ei, haaw! Ei, haaw! Ei, haaw! Ei, haaw!

Storyteller:
He stared and stared,
hungrily.
Raven hadn't eaten for days.
He could hear his stomach growling.
[Raven makes sound of stomach
    rumble.]
He could almost taste the salmon.
He thought,
"How could I get the salmon
to come in?"
Then he found a greenstone.
He brushed it off
and turned it this way and that way.
An idea!
"I'll put this up on a stump!"
Then Raven said,
"Hey, you! You dirty guy!
Listen to what this Greenstone

is saying about you.
Hey, you!
Listen to what he's saying!"

Chorus:
Ei, haaw! Ei, haaw! Ei, haaw! Ei, haaw!

Storyteller:
King Salmon jumped out there.
Raven, yelling at Salmon,
"Hey, you!
Listen to what this little Greenstone
is saying about you.
Listen!"
King Salmon jumped out there,
out from the beach Raven was on.

Chorus:
Ei, haaw! Ei, haaw! Ei, haaw! Ei, haaw!

Storyteller:
Raven starts yelling insults.
"Hey, you!
Listen to what Greenstone said.
Come on ashore!
Come, jump on the beach!"

Chorus:
Ei, haaw! Ei, haaw! Ei, haaw! Ei, haaw!

Storyteller:
And King Salmon
jumped up on the beach.
Raven,
in his foolishness
and short-sighted exploit,
forgot he should have had a club

to hit the nose
of King Salmon.
So he told King Salmon,
"Oh, my! Pardner,
let me go in the woods first.
I can hardly stand it!"
So he ran up in the woods
to get a club.
When he came back down,
he had his club.
But King Salmon
was out in the bay again,
jumping around.

Chorus:
Ei, haaw! Ei, haaw! Ei, haaw! Ei, haaw!

Storyteller:
He jumped out there.
Raven: "Hey!
Listen to what Greenstone
is saying about you!
You dirty mouth!
You dirty-gilled person, you!
Hey! Do you hear this?"
Salmon jumped out there,
not bothered.

Chorus:
Ei, haaw! Ei, haaw! Ei, haaw! Ei, haaw!

Storyteller:
Raven: "Here's what he just said.
You dirty-spined salmon."
At this the salmon
jumped on the beach
by Raven.

As it jumped on the beach
Raven attacked it
with the club.
He slammed the club on its nose
again and again and again and again
until it was gone.

Scene 2

Storyteller:
The salmon was too heavy for him,
so Raven organized
a group of birds
called Alaska Native Birds.
Their acronym
is ANB.
Raven said to them,
"Hey, grandchildren.
Help me pull this salmon up,
and we'll bake it."
When they pulled it up, Raven said,
"We have to dig a pit for the salmon."
They dug up a huge pit.
Then Raven said, "Gee!
Now we gotta get some skunk cabbage
to wrap our salmon with,
and so we can put some skunk cabbage
on the bottom of the fire pit.
Why don't you go and get some?"
Birds: "Let's pick only the nice ones.
That guy is a nice guy."
They went and picked nice huge ones,
nice clean ones,
and hurried back with them.

113

Nora Marks Dauenhauer

Then Raven asked them,
"Let me see."
They piled them up in front of him.
Then he looked them over.
While he looked them over
he asked,
"Where did you pick them?"
They all pointed to the same place
behind the village.
Raven exploded,
"Yuck! Yuck! Yuck! Yuck!
It's contaminated there!
It's as bad as PCBs.
When my wife was alive
she used to go over there!
Throw them away!
They're not fit
to wrap the salmon in!
Throw them away!
Throw them away!
Look at the brown spots on them!"
He was pointing to imaginary spots
    on them.
The little birds were sad
but they still wanted to help Raven.
Birds: "We'll get better ones,
and clean ones too."
Raven told them,
"Go over two mountains.
Get the skunk cabbage
only from there."
Birds: "How could we know
that his wife used to go there?
We should have asked."

They left.
Birds: "Let's hurry.
Salmon is fresh
for only a while."
They hiked.
In the meantime
Raven put the layers of skunk cabbage
and the salmon over them
on the bottom of the pit
the birds had dug for him.
He covered it
and built a fire over it.
When it was done
Raven ate
to his heart's content.
Once in a while
he would burp a long one.
You see,
it's OK to burp
at a Tlingit dinner.
So he ate and ate
and burped and burped
until he ate up
the whole salmon
("Oops! I ate it all!")
before the birds could have any.
He was content.
All that was left was the tail.
He put his craft to work.
He tried to roll a stump
over the fire.
He couldn't.
So he finally just stuck
the tail under it.

He said
"There!"
When the birds came back
Raven was sitting
by the uprooted tree stump
looking sad and saying,
"We're so unlucky, you guys!
This tree stump
rolled over on the salmon
on the fire
and we can't even salvage
any of it!
We've lost all of it!
It's all gone!
All the skunk cabbage
were brought for nothing."
Only the tail
was sticking out
from under the stump.
The birds were sad.
They cried.
The birds were wailing.
All the birds were crying
"Waaaaaaaaaa!"
Some were angry.
Raven was in a fix.
He thought,
"What am I going to do?"
An idea!
Raven: "Hey! You guys!
Why are you crying?
Come here!"
Robin came over.
Robin was cold

and got too close to the fire.
When her belly caught fire
she didn't even feel it
until it was red.
Robin: "Ouch! I'm burning!"
Chickadee was crying.
She rubbed her eyes.
She was so upset while she cried
she rubbed her eyes
and the top of her head.
She rubbed in the soot
she had all over her
from the ashes she was sitting in.
"I'm tired and hungry," she said.
Blue Jay was so angry she went on,
"Yakidi, yakidi, yakidi, yakidi, yak!
You should have cooked the salmon
more carefully!
You should not have built
the fire there
near the stump!"
Raven pulled Blue Jay's feathers
around his head
into a topknot
or a bow.
Raven: "You shouldn't be squawking!
Look at what a nice looking guy you are!
You look funny angry!"
Magpie was trying to fly off
but Raven pulled him back
and tried to calm him down
by running his claws
down his tail.
That's why Magpie

Nora Marks Dauenhauer

has a forked tail.
This is where the chickadee
got its black top
and black rings around the eye.
Robin burned her belly
trying to get at the fire.
Blue Jay still has the comb
Raven made for him
and is still angry
he didn't get any salmon.
What happened to Raven?
After he smooth-talked
the Alaska Native Birds
he realized he had been so busy for
    so long
he worked up an appetite.
You could hear his stomach growling.

Chorus:
Grrrroowwwwlllllllll!

Storyteller:
He quickly grabbed
King Salmon's tail and said,
"I think I'll go see
my brother-in-law, Brown Bear."
And he flew away.

Chorus:
Raven song, *"Du yaa kanagoodi."*

5. How to Make Good Baked Salmon from the River

for Simon Ortiz, and for all our friends
and relatives who love it

It's best made in dryfish camp
on a beach by a fish stream
on sticks over an open fire,
or during fishing
or during cannery season.

In this case, we'll make it in the city,
baked in an electric oven on a black
    fry pan.

INGREDIENTS
Bar-b-q sticks of alder wood.
In this case the oven will do.
Salmon: River salmon,
current supermarket cost
$4.99 a pound.
In this case, salmon poached from river.
Seal oil or hooligan oil.
In this case, butter or Wesson oil,
if available.

DIRECTIONS
To butcher, split head up the jaw.
    Cut through.
Remove gills. Split from throat down
    the belly.
Gut, but make sure you toss all to
    the seagulls

Nora with daughter, Le Florendo, and grandson, Philip, admiring a rack of salmon strips from fish Philip caught and smoked near Juneau, Alaska, mid 1980s.

and the ravens, because they're your kin,
and make sure you speak to them
while you're feeding them.
Then split down along the backbone
and through the skin.
Enjoy how nice it looks when it's split.

Push stake through flesh and skin
like pushing a needle through cloth,
so that it hangs on stakes
while cooking over fire made from
      alder wood.

Then sit around
and watch the slime on the salmon
begin to dry out. Notice how red the
      flesh is,
and how silvery the skin looks.
Watch and listen
how the grease crackles, and smell
      its delicious
aroma drifting around on a breeze.

Mash some fresh berries to go along
      for dessert.
Pour seal oil in with a little water.
      Set aside.

In this case, put the poached salmon
      in a fry pan.
Smell how good it smells while it's
      cooking,
because it's sooooooooooooo important.

Cut up an onion. Put in a small dish.
      Notice
how nice this smells too,
and how good it will taste.
Cook a pot of rice to go along with
      salmon.
Find some soy sauce to put on rice,
or maybe borrow some.

In this case, think about how nice the
      berries
would have been after the salmon,
but open a can
of fruit cocktail instead.

Then go out by the cool stream
and get some skunk cabbage,
because it's biodegradable,
to serve the salmon from.
Before you take back the skunk cabbage,
you can make a cup out of one
to drink from the cool stream.

In this case, plastic forks,
paper plates and cups will do,
and drink cool water from the faucet.

Nora Marks Dauenhauer

TO SERVE

After smelling smoke and fish and
    watching
the cooking, smelling the skunk cabbage
and the berries mixed with seal oil,
when the salmon is done,
put salmon on stakes on the skunk
    cabbage
and pour some seal oil over it
and watch the oil run
into the nice cooked flaky flesh
which has now turned pink.

Shoo mosquitoes off the salmon,
and shoo the ravens away,
but don't insult them, because
    mosquitoes
are known to be the ashes of the
    cannibal giant,
and Raven is known to take off
with just about anything.

In this case, dish out on paper plates
from fry pan. Serve to all relatives
    and friends
you have invited to the bar-b-q
and those who love it.

And think how good it is
that we have good spirits
that still bring salmon and oil.

TO EAT

Everyone knows that you can eat
just about every part of the salmon,
so I don't have to tell you
that you start from the head,
because it's everyone's favorite.
You take it apart,
bone by bone,
but be sure you don't miss
the eyes,
the cheeks,
the nose,
and the very best part—
the jawbone.

You start on the mandible
with a glottalized alveolar fricative
    action
as expressed in the Tlingit verb als'óos.'

Chew on the tasty, crispy skins
before you start on the bones.
Eiiiiiiii!!!!!!
How delicious.

Then you start on the body
by sucking on the fins
with the same action.
Include the crispy skins, and then
the meat with grease oozing all over it.

Have some cool water from the stream
with the salmon.

In this case,
water from the faucet will do.
Enjoy how the water tastes sweeter
    with salmon.

When done, toss the bones to
    the ravens

and seagulls, and mosquitoes,
but don't throw them in the salmon
    stream
because the salmon have spirits
and don't like to see the remains
of their kin thrown in by us
among them in the stream.

In this case, put bones in plastic bag
to put in dumpster.

Now settle back to a story-telling
    session
while someone feeds the fire.

In this case,
small talk and jokes with friends will do
while you drink beer.
If you shouldn't drink beer,
tea or coffee will do nicely.

Gunalchéesh for coming to my bar-b-q.

(6. Salmon Egg Puller—$2.15 an Hour)

You learn to dance with machines,
keep time with the header.

Swing your arms,
reach inside the salmon cavity
with your left hand,
where the head was.

Grab lightly
top of egg sack
with fingers,
pull gently, but quick.
Reach in immediately with right hand
for the lower egg sack.
Pull this gently.

Slide them into a chute to catch
    the eggs.
Reach into the next salmon.
Do this four hours in the morning
with a fifteen-minute coffee break.

Go home for lunch.
Attend to kids, and feed them.
Work four hours in the afternoon
with a fifteen minute coffee break.
Go home for dinner.
Attend to kids, and feed them.

Go back for two more hours,
four more hours.
Reach,
pull gently.

When fingers start swelling,
soak them in epsom salts.
If you don't have time,
stand under a shower
with your hands up under the spray.
Get to bed early if you can.
Next day, if your fingers are sore,
start dancing immediately.
The pain will go away
after icy fish with eggs.

Nora Marks Danenhauer

NORA MARKS DAUENHAUER
(Tlingit) is a poet, writer and keeper
of the flame of Tlingit culture and
language. She has co-written and co-
edited, with husband Richard Dauenhauer, many books about the language
and culture, including *Haa Twunaagu Yis,
For Healing our Spirit: Tlingit Oratory,* for
which the Dauenhauers won an American Book Award. She has been recognized with many other awards such as
the Governor's Award for the Arts, and
was named Humanist of the Year by
the Alaska Humanities Forum.

Nora Marks Dauenhauer
and Richard Dauenhauer,
September, 1996.

She was born in Juneau, Alaska and
raised in that area, in Hoonah, as well as
on the family fishing boat and seasonal
subsistence sites around Icy Straits,
Glacier Bay and Cape Spencer. Her first
language is Tlingit and when she was a
child she says her family spoke English
only when they went to Juneau to make
business deals. Her family held to traditional ceremonial life long after others
had abandoned it, though, she notes,
her father was all for technology in
terms of tools, fishing gear and boats.

Ms. Dauenhauer has taught at the
University of Alaska at Juneau as well as
other schools in Alaska. She is widely
published and internationally recognized for her fieldwork, transcription,
translation and explication of Tlingit
oral literature.

She has four children, twelve grand-
children, and two great grandchildren.
Her book of prose, poetry and plays,
Learning to Dance with Machines, is forth-
coming from University of Arizona
Press.

 ## Ito Oda

in conversation with Tomo Matsui

Traveling by Dugout on the Chitose River and Sending the Salmon Spirits Home: Memoir of an Ainu Woman

Translated by
Jane Corddry Langill
with Rie Taki

The following is an excerpt from the book Hi no Kami no Futokoro nite *(In the Bosom of the Fire God), recollections by Ainu elder Ito Oda, as told to Tomo Matsui. Mr. Matsui interviewed Mrs. Oda in her later years, and he refers to her with respect as "Grandma Ito."*

The story of the life of Ito Oda, born in the early years of this century, not only evokes the traditional Ainu world in which she grew up but also points up the enormous changes in both society and the environment that have taken place in Hokkaido in one lifetime. This chapter describes life on the Chitose River and the importance of salmon in the early days. Mr. Matsui, an editor and scholar, moved to Hokkaido from Tokyo to learn more of Ainu culture. He presents the story of Mrs. Oda with the hope that the wisdom of the heart and respect for the natural world shown by her words and way of life will inspire future generations.

This selection makes reference to several features of traditional Ainu life. Inaw were sacred offerings which took many forms but always included carefully shaved willow sticks. Wood carving was a highly developed art and many implements used in everyday life, such as cutting boards and bowls, were beautifully carved. Houses had a special "god window" on the wall closest to the seat of honor at the fire pit: only deities or offerings to them passed through. There was also an outdoor altar for offerings to gods who did not belong indoors. Yukar are the sacred songs, lengthy epics about heroes or gods chanted around the hearth on special occasions. They served to provide lessons in history and morality as well as entertainment. Special tools and ceremonies for handling salmon are described in some detail in the text. The salmon themselves were called kamuy chep, *the sacred fish.*

Today, millions of salmon are "produced" in hatcheries on the Chitose River, and one can easily travel to the area by airplane and automobile. This memoir describes life on the river some seventy years ago, when travel was by dugout and salmon was treated with the reverence it deserved as the fish of the gods.

Grandma Ito's husband was Kiyosaku Oda, known to his family and friends as Hosaku. His was probably the last generation of Ainu who went up into the mountains to hunt bear and carry out such rituals as the *iyomante*, an ancient ceremony for sending the spirit of the bear back to the world of the gods.

Kiyosaku could go out on the river in a dugout canoe and spear a salmon without letting the boat even veer to the side, so skilled was he in handling it.

"Oh, I'm an expert in a boat," he told me. "You know, because I've been in boats since I was a little kid. Like when we had the big rains, I often went out to help people. You're the only one who can do it, they'd say, so go ahead, but be careful. So I'd rescue people who were stranded, or help them move all their belongings upstairs in their barns. Things like that."

When she married, Ito moved to the town of Rankoshi, today known as Katsuragi. It was a prosperous hamlet on the Chitose River, known for its forests of katsura trees (*ranko*). Ito had many relatives in Rankoshi, and as a child she had often visited the village to help out with things like babysitting. Both Ito and her close friend Toyo came as brides to live in the village.

Rankoshi was close to the mountains and not as suitable for cultivating rice in paddies as Kamaka, the village where Ito had grown up. At the time, the region

A giant katsura tree (*ranko*) is honored by Kiyosaku Oda before he harvests it to make a dugout canoe.

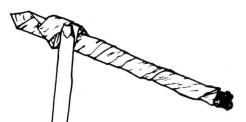

was blanketed with deep forests of giant trees, and the only road was a barely passable, winding path to Lake Shikotsu. It was much easier to come and go by dugout. Perhaps because of that, the river still teemed with fish and people still followed the old mountain ways, going up into the forests to hunt bear and deer. Life was lived much as it had been from ancient times.

"The roads around here were really just narrow paths around and between the big trees that covered the land. We didn't use a horse cart much—we went almost everywhere by boat. Horsecarts made it through when they built that salmon hatchery up the Chitose River, but until then it was just dense bush everywhere.

"In the old days, there were a lot of crabs in the river. In the fall, in corn-eating season, we'd tie a corncob on a string and put it in the water. Pretty soon we'd pull it up with five or six crabs holding onto it! It wasn't very hard to fill up a whole bucket. And they were delicious! Now the crabs and the bullhead and the loach are all gone but there were lots of them in the old days.

"To catch crabs, we'd look down into the water and see them all crawling

Chinoyetat: Torch made of rolled birch bark.

along on the bottom. We'd just pin one down and then toss it into the boat. We took birch bark and made torches, so we could catch the ones walking around on the river bottom. It was really fun. My husband especially enjoyed this, so he'd go out a lot, you know, and take the kids with him."

Imagine this scene. Just as twilight settles over the river, they light a torch of rolled birch bark, load the children into the dugout, and quietly move out onto the water, Kiyosaku handling the boat and Ito holding up the torch. The Chitose River runs fairly swiftly at this point, but Kiyosaku deftly maneuvers the heavy, narrow dugout upstream, wielding just a single oar at the stern. The light of the torch shimmers on the surface of the river, bent into shapes by the ripples. They can look down through the clear water to the bottom of the river and see fish and crabs every-where. The delighted children reach down to catch crabs and toss them into the boat. Giant katsura trees on the banks seem to float up out of the dark-ness. This image speaks with the voice of ancient times, across the centuries.

"Now with the bullhead trout, we'd grill it and make a soup stock. It was really delicious. We also used fish like loach for soup. If we were expecting company, they'd tell us to 'go catch

Ito Oda ✦ Tomo Matsui

some bullhead,' and in an hour we could catch twenty or thirty of them. We'd broil them up for the guests. There were plenty of those lamprey eels, too, but I could never eat *them.*"

As autumn changed to winter, the great luxury for the family was taking up a special spear called a *marep* and going out to fish for salmon. In the fall, the river churned with the returning fish. In those days, of course, it was considered poaching to take any fish from the river, but we cannot expect people to give up what has been a long tradition, handed down from their ancestors. So they waited until sunset to slip out onto the river in a dugout and spear the salmon.

"The salmon's tails were all raggedy and their fins torn up by the time they made it up the river. We also liked the salmon roe, so we would salt it, boil some potatoes, and mix it all together. Oh, that was delicious!

"Hosaku really knew how to use that *marep.* One time, he got a burn on his ankle, and he couldn't wear any shoes. He couldn't even wear a sock. So he bandaged up the ankle, put a wooden clog on the bare foot and a boot on the other one, and went out fishing in his boat anyway, with only one good foot! I guess he really loved fishing. That's why he was so good at it.

"After he caught the salmon, we'd split it open. We could dry it, salt it, or freeze it for *ruipe.* To make *ruipe,* we'd clean the salmon really well to get all the blood out, and hang it up outdoors in the shade to freeze. When winter came, it would freeze very hard, and by the dead of winter, we had them hanging all around the place outside. To eat it, we'd slice off a piece, thaw it out, and then grill it a little bit, just on the skin side."

Occasionally, someone would be caught poaching by the police, causing quite a stir. One fall, Kiyosaku had worked with the local police to build a small jail for poachers, so when a policeman friend caught *him* in the act of poaching, he had an awkward time of it. Kiyosaku told this funny story.

"In bayonet practice I went up against a policeman, and I was the stronger. So we became friends, and I got along very well with him . . . a fellow named Tanaka.

"One time I was out poaching and I'd just caught three fish. Well, I had to urinate, so I brought the boat back to the bank. I sent Ito home with the fish while I went to the toilet. Just as I came out, along came Tanaka from the police. 'Hey, Oda!' 'Yes?' 'You got a boat?' he asked, so I said 'Yeah, I do.'

"I knew this wasn't gonna go too well, but he said, 'Let me see it.' So I took him over to my boat.

"Of course there were no fish in the boat by then, but it was just the time when things freeze over in winter, and he could tell I'd had fish. Three of them, right? Also, I'd left my *marep* in the boat. So he says, 'Do you use this spear to catch fish?' 'Yes, I do.' Then he says, 'Naw, you don't do it, your father does it.' And I say, 'Oh no, I catch them.' 'No, you don't even know how!' he says.

"'That's not true, anybody with a boat like this knows how to catch fish,' I say. 'Here, you handle the boat, and I'll show you how I do it.' 'Don't be ridiculous!' he says, 'You *didn't do it. Your father did it!*' So I said, 'No, I did it. And I'm very sorry.' 'Listen,' he said, 'I ran into you early in the morning, when you had just taken out your spear, get it? So don't go off poaching now.' And I said to him, 'Fine, I understand.'"

It's reassuring to know that at least one policeman had a modicum of human sympathy, but why weren't people allowed to follow their traditions in order to survive?

Today, of course, one cannot even swim in the Chitose River, let alone catch fish. The crabs and the bullhead are all gone. On the lower reaches of the river, the banks are completely cemented over, and fish don't even come near. On the upper reaches of the river, there are plans to log the virgin forests to help with the government's budget problems, so the legendary "pure waters of the Chitose" will soon be clogged with sand and mud. There is also a plan to build a major resort, which many welcome for the sake of development. Living in such an age as this, we have much to learn from the Ainu approach to nature.

◆

In the old days, salmon swimming up the river were welcomed as an important deity and treated with heartfelt reverence. In the Ainu language, one expression for salmon is *kamuy chep*—the fish of the gods. Nowadays, Ainu groups conduct an annual ceremony, called *asir chep nomi* (first fish ceremony), on the banks of the Chitose River to welcome the first salmon home. When I asked Grandma Ito about it, she said that she had no personal recollection of *asir chep nomi* on the Chitose, but she told me about *inawkorchep*, a family ceremony for the first returning salmon. *Inawkorchep* refers to a small salmon, about a foot long, that was selected from the first run of fish returning home in the fall. As Grandma Ito described it, the salmon was adorned with shaved-wood decorations called *inawkike*, and then respectfully and ceremoniously sent back to the land of the gods.

Ito Oda ◆ Tomo Matsui

An elaborate offering (*heper imoka*) for the bear ceremony (*iyomante*) includes shaved willow sticks (*inaw*) and dried salmon.

This first salmon travels back to the land of the gods, decorated with willow shavings and bearing gifts from the human world. Upon arrival, it calls the other gods together and divides up the offerings with them, and these gods note the kindness of the human beings who sent such gifts. In particular, the god who had sent that first salmon to the land of humans is much pleased and promptly sends more fish up the river to that family or village. Grandma Ito described the process for me.

"*Inawkorchep* was just a little fish, you know. Just a little fish that wouldn't even be very good to eat. So instead of eating it we'd decorate it with *inawkike* and send it back home. We called fish like that *inawkorchep,* and they were the fish of the gods.

"It was around September when the first salmon came up the river. I think

the salmon trout were a little earlier. We'd put the salmon on a *nima* and bring into the house. A *nima* is like a cutting board that has been hollowed out. We passed the fish on the board into the house through the god window, carried it to the seat of honor beside the hearth (called the *ape-etok*), and then placed it in the *rotta,* a sacred place in the room next to the seat of honor and closest to the god window. We made offerings for the *inawkorchep* to take back to the gods. We took little piles of rice and malt for brewing sake, wrapped them up in paper, wrapped the paper up in a bamboo leaf, and tied it all up nicely with shaved wood decorations. It looked like a tiny bale of rice, and we put two of these next to the head of the fish on the carved board. . . .

"When the fish gets to where the gods are, the little bundles become real

Mrs. Ito Oda with her eldest daughter, Seiko, infant son, father-in-law (in uniform) and other relatives.

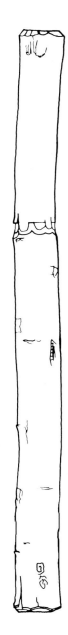

Isapakikni: Special club of willow wood used only for stunning salmon after it was caught.

bales of rice. So they make rice wine with it, I guess, and probably all the gods get together and drink it.

"Along with the little rice bales next to the fish's head, they used to put a lot of the shaved wood decorations right on the fish when they sent it off. I saw my grandpa do that a long time ago. He got a little fish like this, just about a foot long—what we call the *inawkorchep*—and put a lot of the shavings on top, sent it back out of the house through the "god window," and told it to go·back to the land of the gods. It wasn't a very big fish, you know. They put it out on the *inawchipa* (an altar on the outside of the house), so it probably traveled from there up to where the gods are. And that was how we made sure that we would get lots of salmon to catch.

"In the *yukar* epics, the gods send salmon everywhere. And they say that if the gods send them, they'll come. So I guess those fish must be a blessing from the gods, right? I don't know what kind of god the salmon god is, but I bet it doesn't look like a salmon. In the land of the gods, it probably looks more like a person, don't you think?"

We know how important salmon were to the Ainu from the fact that they appear in so many of the old epic stories and sacred chants.

With creatures like deer and salmon

that existed in abundance and were frequently hunted, the gods who sent them to this world in such great numbers were considered to be deities of a higher order. In other words, an individual deer could be sent back to the world of the gods with much less ceremony than could a bear, for example. Nevertheless, all hunted creatures were considered sacred, and it was important to treat each with respect. The traditional tales and epic poems taught children to respect all animals and treat them with courtesy, for they were all sacred.

When a salmon was caught, it was killed with a blow to the head. Ainu used a special tool for this task, the *isapakikni*. This was a ceremonial club made of white wood such as willow and decorated with wood shavings, like the *inaw*. A farm tool or a dirty old stick would never have been used. The salmon willingly gives its life for a human being, proving that it is a sacred spirit. For this, humans must be grateful. To Ainu who lived in the natural world where fishing and hunting were a part of life, the gravity and importance of the act of offering one's life were deeply felt and appreciated.

In the Ainu world view, the rivers were sacred paths climbed by the fish, who were gods.

129

Ito Oda ✦ Tomo Matsui

130

"In the old days we drank the water from the Chitose River. Now it has become a sewer, and the water is too dirty to drink. We used to go down to the river to get our drinking water. Of course there were wonderful fish then, too, and we treasured them.

"We never washed our laundry in the river, either. We were taught that it would be rude to the gods. Instead, we scooped water into a bucket and took the laundry up into the hills. Up there, we made sure that it got good and clean. We really treated the river carefully."

This attitude of respect, reverence and gratitude to the gods was alive in everyone's hearts in those times. With gods at the center of their everyday existence, human beings lived in harmony with the natural world, enjoying its abundance. The Ainu did not pollute the natural world of Hokkaido—the rivers, the forests, the mountains, the ocean or the air. Rather, they recognized it as the land of the gods and treated it with respect.

(Translated from Japanese.)

ITO ODA (Ainu) was born in Umaoi, Chitose City, Hokkaido in 1911. A respected Ainu elder (*fuchi*), she is one of the few living informants on traditional culture and values. When she was three years old, her family moved to Kamaka to farm. She lost her father soon thereafter and went to work at the age of ten, providing the main income for her family.

Mrs. Oda remembers her childhood well. When work was done at the end of the day and everyone sat around the hearth in a dark house, she saw the figure of her grandmother as *Apefuchikamuy*, the god of fire, watching over her, as her mother and ladies of the village recited epic poems. She also witnessed many of the *kamuy nomi*, celebrations to communicate with the gods conducted throughout the seasons. In her later years, she shared precious knowledge of Ainu customs with writer Tomo Matsui to create the book *Hi no Kami no Futokori nite* (In the Bosom of the Fire God). She has been an active member of the Chitose Ainu Culture Preservation Society and a teacher in the Chitose Ainu Language School. Today she lives in Katsuragi with her children.

TOMO MATSUI (Japanese) was born in Tokyo in 1953. After completing a master's degree at Sophia University in Tokyo in 1979, he enrolled in Salzburg University in Austria, where he pursued an interest in philosophy and cosmology through the study of Goethe, Jung and other German thinkers. On his return to Japan, he directed his interest in cosmology to the Ainu world view. As editor-in-chief of Fukutake Press (today called Benesse), he oversaw the publication of many books for children about Ainu culture. In 1991, he met Ito Oda by chance when he bought the land for his house in Katsuragi. Through Mrs. Oda's descriptions of her life, he gained an understanding of the universality of the Ainu world view. Convinced that her experience and wisdom would be useful to readers everywhere, he worked with her to prepare the book *Hi no Kami no Futokoro nite*, excerpted here.

Ito Oda ◆ Tomo Matsui

SANDRA OSAWA

The Makah Indians

We sprang from salt water
a meeting of waves.
Our men hollowed
canoes
from logs
with the bone of whale
and together we rose
as one
but were many
giving thanks to the sea
with a song.
We were born
startling the birds
into flight
while the seagulls
cried
circling the air
and following the strain of our paddles
moving us
toward land.

Now our men keep
returning
to the sea
filled with the rhythm of salmon
flashing a strange beauty
through dark waters
as silver fins
leap wildly over death
seeking the savage moment
that saves
the young.
Our people will not die.

The Politics of Taking Fish

There is a striking parallel between the salmon as they struggle upstream to spawn and the tribes of the Northwest as they struggle to retain their treaty right to fish. Both continue to meet and overcome great obstacles and the most common threat to them both has been politics. When conflicts have arisen over this past century, it is usually the salmon and the tribes that have lost out to the more powerful political interests of big business, timber, railroad, mining, farming and hydroelectric power.

One arena where both the tribes and the salmon began winning, however, is in the courts, particularly the United States Supreme Court. It will surprise many to know that court battles over fishing began very early and have continued to the present day. Tribes have persistently fought for the continued right to fish for over 150 years and what becomes clear is that a way of life was at stake, a tradition and a culture. Even though much of our way of life has been lost, this right to fish has never been surrendered.

In the very beginning there was fish . . . and fish aplenty. Lewis and Clark delineated about 100 fishing stations or lodges along the Columbia. "The multitude of this fish," noted Clark, "is almost inconceivable. The water is so clear that they can readily be seen at a depth of 115 or 120 feet. But at this season they float in such quantities down the stream the Indians have only to collect, split and dry them on the scaffolds."

Ezra Meeker who came to Puget Sound in the early 1850s noted, "fish abounded in all the streams at that season of the year and if interrupted at one place the women could find the salmon abundant elsewhere." Speaking of the headwaters of the short creek emptying into the Puyallup River, he said, "I have seen the salmon so numerous at the shoalwater of the channel as to literally touch each other. It was utterly impossible to wade across without touching the fish." Many Indian people living today can still remember the days when you could almost walk across the rivers on the backs of the fish.

The first contacts between the early explorers and the tribes of the Northwest was not necessarily hostile. The first explorers were in need of food and found the tribes willing to trade for objects they had on board. It is believed that the Northwest Coast Indians captured about thirty-five million pounds of salmon annually at the time of the first European contacts, which testifies to the great importance of salmon in their way of life.

In addition to food and the economy, salmon played an important part in the religious and ceremonial life of the tribes. One aspect of this, which you can still see today, is the first salmon ceremony. In this ceremony, the bones of the first salmon caught are carefully returned to the river amidst prayers that the salmon will return and multiply. The Skokomish, the Lummi, the Tulalip, the Klickitat and the Yakama are a few of the tribes who still hold these ceremonies each spring.

In the early 1800s, America was busy making treaties with the governments of Spain, Russia and Great Britain in order to extinguish their land claims to this country. When this was done, there was still a problem, for the land claims of the Indians had never been extinguished. Overland expansion in the West began in the 1840s as the first white settlers arrived with the creation of the Oregon Territory. The Territorial Act of 1848 specifically preserved the rights and property of the Indians. This meant that by law only the U.S. could deal with the tribes. Anxious to avoid probable hostilities, the U.S. assigned Washington Territorial Governor Isaac Stevens to begin the treaty-making process that would extinguish legal title to the land and hasten settlement in the West.

At the time of the treaties the tribes had increased their fishing in order to meet the demands of the settlers for food and trade. The early explorers were more interested in the animal pelts than the fish, at least initially. An 1854 letter from Governor Stevens notes, "The Indians on Puget Sound have been for a considerable time in contact with the whites. . . . They form a very considerable proportion of the trade of the Sound. They catch most of our fish, supplying not only our people with clams and oysters, but salmon to those who cure and export it."

It was in this context that Stevens began his whirlwind mission with the tribes of Washington. On this mission, he encountered a persistent response. Men rose in treaty council proceedings to express their concern over the need to keep fishing. It has accurately been said that while the white man wanted the right to the land, the Indian wanted his right to the water. Tse-Kaw-Wooth from Ozette in the treaty of Neah Bay is reported to have said that he wanted the sea, this was his country. Thus, a

135

Sandra Osawa

Ellen + mother   Jimmy   Petíe   Capt John

Rare photo of Sandra Osawa's Makah relatives, circa 1870. Far right is Osawa's great great-grandfather, a signer of the Makah treaty.

non-controversial clause was part of the treaty. In return for the tribes ceding vast areas of their present land, it was stipulated that, "The right of taking fish at all usual and accustomed places is further secured to said tribes in common with the citizens of the territory." This was the clause that was later to be debated and contested and that was to find its way up to the U.S. Supreme Court seven times for a definitive interpretation. Yet at the time it was inserted, it seemed only a clause meant to appease the tribes, since the treaty was motivated by a quest for land, not fish.

In 1855 and as late as 1870, there was no non-Indian fishery developed of any consequence. Non-Indian interests were still largely with agriculture and timber. Indeed in the first state legislature in 1889, there was only one congressman who listed his vocation as a fishermen. Almost half were attorneys and farmers. Soon after treaties had been signed with the tribes in five major areas, Stevens issued word through the Oregon and Washington papers that the territories were now open for settlements. Although the treaties would not be ratified for years, such news set off a frenzy of settlers who began moving onto what was still Indian land.

Ollie Mason of the Quinault Tribe noted that the settlers began casting envious eyes at the Quinault fishery and asking if the Quinaults could be pushed a little further off their lands. Mason said "the ink wasn't even yet dry on the treaties, when they began asking us to move a little further up the river. . . ." Mason's great grandfather was Chief Taholah, who signed the treaty and heard first-hand the promise that their fishing rights would be protected. The stories of their subsequent struggles were passed down to each generation and Mason's grandfather told him that "we will always have to struggle to keep our fishing rights, always have to struggle to keep our fishing rights."

If fishing was largely an unimportant activity to the whites, it did not long remain so. Warnings about the decline of the Pacific Coast salmon are not new and came as early as the 1890s. The first report of the Oregon Game and Fish Protector issued an urgent warning in 1894, "It does not require a study of statistics to convince one that the salmon industry has suffered a great decline during the past decade, and that it is only a matter of a few years under present conditions when the Chinook of the Columbia will be as scarce as the

beaver that was once so plentiful in our streams. . . . For a third of a century, Oregon has drawn wealth from her streams, but now by reason of her wastefulness and lack of intelligent provision for the future, the source of that wealth is disappearing and is threatened with annihilation."

Cannery growth had begun on the Columbia River and had spread to Puget Sound, where the first cannery was built in 1877. By 1905, there were twenty-four canneries on Puget Sound. Non-Indian fishing interests grew by leaps and bounds and in 1895, Commissioner Crawford of Washington State noted, "The people are just now awakening to the value of the fish of Puget Sound and industry has almost doubled."

In these early days, gear was limited to drift gill nets or seines, some of which were pulled by horses. There were also some set nets, patterned after the Indian's use of nets. Fish traps and fish wheels played the largest and most dominant role, however, and by 1897, traps owned by canneries and large investors dominated the industry. Trolling did not begin off Oregon until 1912 and by 1920, the trolling fleet had swollen to a thousand boats.

The first major litigation regarding the treaty right came in 1887 in U.S. vs. Taylor, when Washington was still a

Sandra Osawa

territory. Four Yakamas named Wyniar, Stylux, Benson and Bill Sehiam were prevented from reaching the Tumwater fishing site on the Columbia River because Taylor, a white homesteader, had constructed a fence. The U.S. joined with the Yakama Indians in their complaint that they were prevented from reaching their "usual and accustomed" fishing site, which was guaranteed by treaty. The Supreme Court of the territory ruled in favor of the Indians, citing the treaty and the existence of certain ancient fisheries which had for generations been used by the Indians.

Although the treaty right to fish was legally upheld and recognized as early as 1887, in practice it was disregarded. A familiar pattern was to develop as tribes saw that winning in court did not necessarily mean winning in practice.

Just eleven years after U.S. vs. Taylor, the Lummi Indians were chased at gunpoint off their usual and accustomed fishing sites at Semiahmoo Spit. Only forty-three years earlier, the Lummis at the Point No Point Treaty had voiced their concerns about their possible loss of food if they signed the treaty, saying, "Our food is berries, deer, and salmon. . . . Where shall we find these? I am afraid I shall become destitute and perish for want of food." These fears of being blocked from their fishing sites were to be realized too soon. The guns and the political wishes of the settlers were stronger than the treaty. Soon the law of the state was also used to invalidate federal treaties—a practice which was illegal but which was to continue through most of this century.

The tribe brought suit against the cannery owners in U.S. vs. Alaska Packers Association (1897), but lost. The judge supported the growth of business and thought the tribe could actually benefit by selling their fish to them. This was strange logic, considering that the tribe was losing one of their prime fishing locations. Since the State of Washington had granted the fish wheel owners a license to fish at Point Roberts, the judge held they had a legal right to be there. At this point in time, state judges in particular had no idea that when a state law conflicts with a federal law, that state law is simply wrong. The presiding judge, Judge Hanford, was to deny many tribal fishing cases and often the tribes did not have the resources to appeal to a higher court. Captain Jack and Hillaire Crockett brought this suit for the Lummis, and many other Lummis helped testify. Some who testified were actually present at the time of the treaty-making sessions in 1855. General Gaines, a Lummi, testified in the Circuit Court by saying, "I was at Mukilteo when Governor Stevens made the treaty with our people in 1855. . . . Our headmen told Governor Stevens that *Chiltenum* (Point Roberts) was their best fishing grounds and they wanted to know whether if they signed the paper they could fish there, and he told them he would put it down on the paper that they could go to Point Roberts just as they had always done. . . ." The promises did get put down on paper, but in practice the promises were ignored, especially as salmon became more and more profitable for non-Indians.

With statehood in 1889 came a more organized campaign aimed at restricting the treaty right to fish. In 1890, the legislature outlawed salmon fishing in most of Northern Puget Sound during March, April and May. This halted the traditional Indian saltwater harvest of spring Chinooks. Later the legislature prohibited spearing, gaffing, snagging and snaring fish, curtailing traditional means of Indian fishing. The 1887 Commissioner of Indian Affairs report for the Tulalip agency noted that the state imposed a tax on all people fishing with a net and also banned the use of nets within 240 feet of any fish trap. This was a direct assault on Indian fishing methods. In 1897, the legislature closed river fishing within Puget Sound and saltwater fishing within three miles of

the mouths of all tributaries. This did not apply to an Indian who took fish for himself and family, but did interfere with traditional Indian fishing for trade and sale. In 1899, the state legislature further closed all rivers and streams to salmon fishing for two months and also totally closed six rivers to salmon fishing. All of these rivers were usual and accustomed grounds for a number of treaty tribes.

But weren't such restrictions helpful, even if the treaty right was damaged? Economists Crutchfield and Pontcorvo in discussing this early period of state regulation between 1890 and 1921 said, "As best we can determine from the dim record, most of the regulations promulgated were based on an intuitive feeling that certain types of gear were excessively destructive or were undertaken in response to the interests of one pressure group or another."

Anthony Netboy, noted writer and salmon authority, also mentions the absence of biological and environmental information in determining early fishery regulations, noting that "Seldom, if ever, were the eroding effects of civilization or the freshwater environment considered as factors in the decreasing abundance of fish."

Early state restrictions were aimed at restricting fishing at river sites, affecting

Sandra Osawa

the traditional fishing sites of the tribes who ran primarily a terminal fishery, so called because it was located at the end of the salmon's life cycle. This was a state practice which was to continue until ordered by the Federal Court to do otherwise. Since tribes were often at the end of the line in terms of a chance at the fish, it was easy to regulate the salmon so that everybody else got their chance first. With fewer and fewer salmon returning back to the rivers, after being intercepted elsewhere, the tribes found themselves virtually squeezed out of the fishery.

As early as 1900, we have fisheries officials pointing their finger at the tribes, asserting that treaty rights might destroy the state hatchery runs. Calls for hatchery construction in the 1890s and the concern over hatchery production make it obvious that people knew the resource was in trouble. A license fee was put on fish wheels, traps and certain nets for hatchery construction. There was hope that hatcheries would help restore the fishery and those hopes were to continue even after the 1930s when a federal study helped show that present hatchery methods were doing little to help restore the runs. Official policy has continued to promote hatcheries up to the present time. It seems it was easier to consider a Band-Aid approach, rather than to address the real reasons behind the declining salmon resource.

In 1905 there came the second most important litigation to uphold the treaty right to fish. Winans, owner of four fish wheels, had placed them along the Columbia River bank where Yakamas had traditionally fished. Winans, a non-Native, blocked Chief White Swan and Thomas Simpson and others from reaching their usual and accustomed fishing sites and the tribe brought suit. The Supreme Court upheld their right and found that their right to resort to the fishing places was "not much less necessary to the existence of the Indians than the atmosphere they breathed."

It was to become more and more difficult to breathe, however, as the century moved into the roaring twenties. The state legislature again closed Puget Sound tributaries above the tide line to fishing, except by hook and line. Since most tribal fisherman used nets, this adversely affected the tribes. Fifty-two years earlier, the tribes had agreed to share the fishing right with the whites and now found themselves restricted and virtually excluded from the fishery.

Three state court decisions in 1916 followed up the attack on the Indian treaty right, suggesting that tribes no longer had a legal right to fish outside reservations, except as permitted by

Makah carver at
Neah Bay.

with the powerful Seufert brothers and their cannery and fish wheel operations. Williams accused Seufert of trying to run him off his usual and accustomed fishing place and he won his case at the U.S. Supreme Court level in 1916.

Even with court victories like Winans and Seufert, the number of non-Indian fishermen continued to increase. In the mid-1920s, political battles began between gill-netters, trollers, purse seiners and trap owners as they sought to obtain a bigger piece of the fish pie, only the pie was shrinking and continued to decline from 1921 to 1945.

There were a few cries of alarm about the unlimited growth of both sport and commercial fleets, but nothing was done. State actions, however, continued to adversely affect the treaty right as salmon preserves outlawed commercial fishing in some areas, outlawing Indian marine fishing by a dozen tribes. Laws during this early period, usually left the sportsman unrestricted as his political clout grew. In 1925 the state gave a whole species of fish, the steelhead, over to the sole use of one group of people—sports fishermen. The winter food of the tribes was gone. This was the same species that was running in the rivers at the time Governor Stevens waved the signed treaty over his head and said, "This paper secures your fish." The paper

state law. One state court opinion was particularly scathing in its attack, saying, "The premise of Indian sovereignty we reject. The treaty is not to be interpreted in that light. . . . At no time did our ancestors, in getting title to this continent, ever regard the aborigines as other than mere occupants of the soil, and incompetent occupants of the soil. Any title that could be had from them was always disdained. . . . Only that title was esteemed that came from white men." (Washington State vs. Townessnut, 1916) Racism was rampant, even in a court of law.

The tribes continued to win in the higher courts, even as they lost in the lower ones. Sam Williams, an Indian Shaker minister, was one of the few Indians to own a fish wheel on the Columbia River. He soon became entangled

Sandra Osawa

or the treaty had secured very little, little but personal and political battles in a long political journey to obtain justice and to enforce the word of the United States government.

To make political matters worse, in 1933 a separate game department was established to serve the interest of one group and was soon to become the most aggressive opponent of the treaty right to fish.

As testimony to their political strength, the sportsmen grouped with the purse seiners to introduce a measure, Initiative 77, to ban the use of fish traps. The highly visible traps were thought to be depleting the runs.

In retrospect, Initiative 77 of 1934 solved nothing. The declining catch was simply redistributed among the remaining user groups. In 1937 the Washington Director of Fisheries stated with regard to the Chinook and coho, "It is evident that the trollers and purse seiners are still taking a serious toll on the fish outside the jurisdiction of the state in the ocean and that they together with the sportsman are more responsible for the depletion of this species than were the fish traps."

Fishing intensity was to continue to increase while in the few years after 1935, all groups doubled their gear. Fishing growth continued growing by

leaps and bounds, naturally to the continued frustration of all, who had not addressed any of the real problems with the dwindling resource. Fish traps were outlawed, yes, and the Indian right to fish had been severely curtailed. But the real culprits in this case were having a field day. Washington State urbanization and industrialization were booming and were allowed to flourish, with no real checks on environmental decay. We were still in the era where little was known about the environment.

Logging interests were allowed to obstruct and pollute the waterways. Monumental wastes were being dumped into the waterways by paper and pulp mills. Serious barriers to the fish were presented as logging companies transported their logs to the mills by water. These holding logs were total blocks to the fish struggling to get up and down the rivers. When railroads came, some of these log dams were simply abandoned, while some remained as permanent barriers to fish movement. Not until 1967 was a comprehensive report published on the effects of pulp and paper pollution. During this study, it was found that around Port Angeles, for example, sulfides and other poisons from three pulp mills were the principle causes of fish mortalities, although untreated sewage didn't help much. The combined report said that all the young test salmon coming into contact with the sluggish water inside Ediz Hook became disoriented and died.

Dams also played havoc on the fish runs. While fish ladders were thought to be the answer, it was later discovered that dams can drastically affect water temperatures and the seasonal flow of water and can contribute to silt, all factors which have an adverse affect on the fish run. Super-saturated nitrogen gas created in reservoirs by heavy water spills over dams is now regarded as the most lethal of all components in dam construction. According to the Washington State Department of Fisheries nitrogen super-saturation alone killed more than five million fish in the Columbia and Snake Rivers in 1971.

We know now that the great decline of salmon and steelhead stocks began about the time the Bonneville and Grand Coulee Dams became operative. Sockeye and chum were virtually eliminated. Two-thirds of the spawning grounds of the Columbia had been destroyed. Again, this was due to the dams, not the tribal fishing right, yet no one protested against dams.

Netboy sums up the disastrous decline of runs on the Columbia by saying, "It has been the victim of our straining after economic progress without paying adequate attention to the effects of hydroelectric projects, nuclear plants, irrigation works, timber cutting and especially the ecological changes that follow in their train." Since it is only recently that the effects of environmental damage have been brought to public attention, it is not surprising that public attention was to remain focused on ways to restrict the tribal right to fish.

In 1939, Sampson Tulee, a Yakama, was arrested for fishing without a state license and convicted in state court. The Supreme Court of the U.S. reversed his conviction, however, saying in 1942, "It is our responsibility to see that the terms of the treaty are carried out so far as possible in accordance with the meaning they were understood to have by tribal representatives at the council."

True to the pattern of the past, the Tulee legal victory did not bring actual victory. In 1947, the White Snohomish, Dungeness and Elwha Rivers were closed to all salmon fishing, posing a heavy restraint on Indian fishing.

In 1950 the Makahs, hurt by the closure of the Hoko River, an off-reservation fishing site, brought suit against Washington, winning in the court of appeals. This case is significant because the court found that the state had not proven that closure of the river was necessary for conservation. The

Sandra Osawa

Racks of fish drying
at Tatoosh Island.

144

courts were beginning to see how politics were influencing the results of who got how much of the dwindling fish pie. Encouraged no doubt by the Makahs, the Puyallups began exercising their right to fish. Bob Satiacum, a Puyallup, challenged the state by fishing the Puyallup, a river which had been closed to Indian fishing since 1907. His dismissal was upheld by the State Supreme Court. The '50s were to be times in which the tribes gained momentum in their move to regain their fishing rights. In 1958, the Umatillas won a case in the court of appeals and the court noted that closing down Indian fishing for conservation purposes was only a state action which sought specifically to protect commercial and sports fishing interests. The regulation, they said, was promulgated with no regard for the welfare of Indians. This

case was significant because, like the Hoko case, the court again noted the political way in which terms like conservation were being used. It noted also the allocation methods used by the state in which fish were effectively allocated away from the tribes. Political manipulation of the fisheries was slowly coming to light.

The turbulent years of the '60s might best be characterized as a time when both sides dug in. Prior cases throughout the century had given tribes a legal foothold, but they had been effectively squeezed out of the fishery. The states of both Washington and Oregon managed the fisheries in such a manner that the tribes were able to take less than three percent of the annual catch. In the '60s, the battle became full blown as the state and tribes battled on the rivers and battled in the courtroom. The Franks Landing area on the Nisqually River served as a catalyst for change with particular credit going to the Al and Maiselle Bridges family. Their family and their three teenage daughters inspired national interest and attention due to their eloquence and strong determination to keep protesting in spite of great personal risks. The state responded with a constant series of raids, arrests and the confiscation of nets and boats that hit the Nisqually, Puyallup and Muckleshoot river people extremely hard. State senators, including Warren G. Magnuson, introduced legislation and held hearings on the idea of purchasing off-reservation fishing rights. The Department of Fisheries repeatedly said the Indian catch took a disproportionately high percent of the spawning runs, fanning public anger. The Puyallups went up to the Supreme Court three times.

Finally, at the end of the turbulent '60s, the Sohappy case in Oregon signaled a clear victory in the recognition of the treaty right. The case was initiated by David Sohappy but became consolidated into a case called U.S. vs. Oregon. Many Indian people prefer to call it the Sohappy case, in honor of David, who fought for over three decades simply for the right to fish. The court emphatically declared that the treaty right guaranteed the Indians a "fair share" of the catch. The court again knocked down Oregon's pattern of allocating the fish away from the tribes. Judge Belloni, the presiding judge, noted "If Oregon intends to maintain a separate status for commercial and sports fisheries, it is obvious a third must be added, the Indian fishery. . . ."

❧

The Indian fishery could easily have been wiped out, were it not for the persistence of people like David Sohappy. His persistence, like that of others before him, was not based simply on an abstract legal concept or on an economic desire. On countless occasions, Sohappy would testify in court and to news reporters as to why he needed to keep fishing the river. It was an explanation that was never understood because David Sohappy was speaking from the perspective of another culture, another time and another religion that no one really understood. He was speaking as a man with a unique relationship with the salmon and he knew that the salmon and his people were as one. Along with this relationship came a special duty and responsibility to remain on the river.

Sohappy was always a thorn in the side of both Washington and Oregon and later to the tribes, who agreed to compromise and work with the states. He became the object of an intensive sting operation that was finally to land him in prison for five years. He noted later that hardened criminals had a hard time understanding why an old man was in prison . . . for fishing. Sohappy was reviled as being greedy, but his role was never really understood. Sohappy lived in a shack along the river and we are not used to holy people, or healers, or

Sandra Osawa

spiritual leaders living in shacks, going fishing. We've forgotten that there was another spiritual leader, who was also a fisherman and who also came from impoverished surroundings. Hauling David Sohappy off to prison was similar to hauling the Pope away from the Vatican. Both had religious duties to perform and both had a sacred place to perform those duties. On one rare occasion I had a chance to talk to David Sohappy and he told me that his prayers helped insure that the salmon would return a thousand fold. He continued that his prayers were *not* just so the Indian could have more fish, but for the very survival of the salmon itself. Gazing into David's worn but still feisty face, I began to understand again why he could never leave the river voluntarily. I understood that when Indian people stop fishing, so too will the fish stop running. When we stop our prayers for the salmon, then we both will truly be finished. I was reminded again of the powerful connection between Indian people and salmon and the powerful dependence one has on the other.

Despite the legal victory of the Sohappy case, the early '70s were still marred by the state's reluctance to change what by now had become a deeply imbedded political philosophy. The Game Department, in particular,

steadfastly refused to allow tribes to gillnet for steelhead. The state still had not acted on the need to curtail the unlimited entry of the fishing fleet, a policy which we know only contributed to the decline of the fish.

Finally, spurred on by the continual protests and backlash at Franks' Landing, the United States sued Washington on behalf of several tribes. This was to be the case that settled the matter once and for all. After three years of exhaustive research, not only was the tribes' treaty right to fish upheld, but it was upheld to the extent that they had the opportunity to take fifty percent of the harvestable catch, not including ceremonial use. A great deal of anthropological evidence was brought to bear on the case as well as definitions of what the words "in common" and "property rights" might have meant to the tribes. The precedence of the past legal decisions also lent support. Belloni's "fair share" ruling in Oregon had suggested that the tribes were not obtaining a fair share of the resource, but it was left to Judge Boldt to determine exactly what that "fair share" would be. The District Court also noted that state fishing regulations have been catastrophic to Indian well-being and implemented a fisheries advisory board to handle forthcoming disputes. The court placed a great deal of weight on biological evidence and scientific data, testimony to the growing importance of managing the fisheries from a scientific rather than a political point of view. This aspect of the ruling continues to be one of the biggest benefits of the famous Boldt Decision.

True to political patterns, however, the court decision found itself frustrated by lack of implementation. Although the state was ordered to cut back on the non-Indian fishery in order to provide for the Indian fishery, the state was unwilling to do so. The state relied on arguments that it could not discriminate in favor of one fishing group at the expense of the other, a surprising argument in light of their past history of discriminatory measures. In 1977, the Washington State Court affirmed that argument and ruled that Washington could not restrict non-treaty fishing in order to make fish available at usual and accustomed places. This was the rallying cry for hundreds of fishermen to fish in open defiance of the District Court orders, clinging instead to this State Court opinion.

The argument was voiced that this should be an equal opportunity fishery, and that tribes shouldn't be given additional fishing time to obtain their share as the court required. The equal opportunity argument also rang hollow, given

the past hundred years of inequality in the fisheries.

Non-Indian hopes were placed on subsequent appeals to the U.S. Supreme Court, which at first refused to hear the case. The lack of acceptance of the district court ruling, the conflicting state and federal court opinions, illegal fishing and political pressure from top levels of government all combined to play a part in the Supreme Court's granting the right to review the decision. At this same time, a federal task force was sent out, presumably to see if they could negotiate an out-of-court settlement. The tribes rightfully wondered why they should settle out of court when they had just won a stunning court victory.

As we know by now, the U.S. Supreme Court upheld the Boldt Decision in 1979. They again noted the district court's opinion that ". . . except for some desegregation cases in the south the district court has faced the most concerted official and private efforts to frustrate a decree of a federal court witnessed this century." The political machinations of the state were openly revealed and struck down. Not surprisingly, this slap at Washington State politics did not make the major newspaper headlines and few people in the country are aware of this embarrassing parallel to the desegregation cases in the South.

Sandra Osawa

Sandra Osawa with
her husband and
collaborator,
Yasu Osawa.

148

The tribes now have a legal right to fifty percent of the harvestable salmon, but it comes at a time when there is very little salmon left. Although the treaty right to fish has been upheld since 1905 in the highest court in this land, it has consistently been denied here at home. Had tribes not been used as scapegoats for the dwindling resource over this past century and had the real problems of resource management been addressed, the tribes, the salmon and our environment would be much stronger today. Perhaps the next century will take a more rational approach toward both the salmon and the tribes.

This century-long struggle to preserve a way of life is one of the most extensive legal battles in this country. Credit must be given to the many tribal people who encountered resistance, but kept fighting, decade after decade. It is wishful thinking to assume that the struggles have ended, but legal gains have been made. If the spirit of David Sohappy continues to live in Indian people who are to follow, our lives as Indian people and as salmon will be brighter. It would be well to remember the warning of a noted salmon authority who said, "an environment in which salmon cannot live, may soon be an environment where man cannot live."

SANDRA OSAWA (Makah) is a writer and independent video producer. She was the first Native American to produce for commercial television with an award-winning information series on Native Americans that aired in 1975 on NBC. She also produced *The Eighth Fire* for NBC and *Lighting the Seventh Fire,* aired on PBS. Her half-hour documentary, *In the Heart of Big Mountain,* aired on the Learning Channel. She produced *Pepper's PowWow,* screened at the 1996 Sundance Film Festival and broadcast nationally on PBS. Her videos have also been featured at the Amtens Film Festival in France, the Vienna Film Festival, the Margaret Mead Film Festival and the Museum of Modern Art's Video Viewpoints.

Sandra led her tribe's War on Poverty program and launched the first Indian Head Start Program in Washington State. She's taught at The Evergreen State College and Seattle Community College. Her articles and poems have been published in newspapers, journals and anthologies. She and her husband and artistic collaborator, Yasu Osawa, own a production company, Upstream Productions in Seattle, where they live with their two children.

Sandra Osawa

Turn of the century
photograph of the
village of Nivo. The
village chief (left)
and the two first
ladies of the town.

VLADIMIR M. SANGI

The Nyvkhs: The People of the Larch

The self-designated name of the people living in the Russian Far East on the Lower Amur River and on Sakhalin Island is Nyvkh. In earlier written records they were known as Gilyami, a name their neighbors, the Manchus, gave them, but they have always called themselves Nyvkhs. Their language belongs to the Paleo-Asiatic group and is unconnected to any other group or the languages of their neighbors, the Ulchi, Orochi or Nanai. Over the centuries Nyvkhs retained their independence from China and Manchu while retaining fruitful trade and cultural relations. They were annexed by the Russian state in the mid-nineteenth century.

A fishing and hunting culture, the Nyvkh shared many ceremonies and beliefs with the Ainu, neighbors to the south, including special reverence for the bear. Nyvkhs have always considered farming a disgraceful injury to the land. The Soviet regime sought to have Nyvkhs leave the sea and become lumbermen or agricultural laborers in collectives. Due to this basic difference in philosophy there has been a great deal of unrest in the Nyvkh areas. From the 1930s through the 1970s the Nyvkhs sought to resist collectivization and resettlement. Fishing villages were officially "closed" in favor of farming communes. Today there are few fishermen left among the Nyvkh.

Following is a story the Nyvkh tell about their origins. It is excerpted from Songs of the Nyvkhs by Vladimir M. Sangi.

At first there was only water. There was no land at all. The duck swam over the water. When the time came for her to give birth she saw her eggs would sink if she laid them on the water. She pulled out her own fluff and made a nest. Her babies grew up strong and healthy. In their own time they made more nests for their own babies. Gradually there got to be so many nests that they joined together and formed an island. This is how the earth began. First grass began to grow on the island and then trees. As tree leaves and needles fell, the island grew into the big land. Then sap came from the larch tree. As its drops struck the ground they turned into people—the Nyvkh, the people of the larch.

As the natural resources of the Nyvkh homeland become further depleted the Nyvkh people struggle to retain their cultural identity.

At The Source

translated by
Valeri Ajaja with
Judith Roche

Poloun got up early. He walked out on the porch and noticed smoke streaming over several houses. It spiraled upward like the smoke from his pipe, isolated from the rest of the world. Thoughts drifted into his head, jammed up and drowned him. Ah, Poloun has missed something important, something that hovers nearby but can't fit into the loop of his thoughts. What is it that depresses the oldest survivor from the Kevongun tribe, the one who has outlived all his relatives? Sometimes this or that ancient event keeps Poloun's mind busy for a long time. He considers his own behavior, and concludes events could have turned out another way if only he had acted differently. Poloun sighed, "Why bother when it happened so long ago."

After the black disease and the raiding, only Poloun and several women were left from his once powerful tribe. He had a bride, but she was taken with most of the other women to a village on the West Coast. Poloun looked for another wife but there were none left. He remained unmarried and over the last sixty-seven winters bitter thoughts piled heavily on his shoulders, bending his back more each year.

Streams of smoke slowly floated up. The sun was stuck somewhere between the mountains but its glow informed the world it was about to appear. A draft broke through the old man's warm chest invigorating his flabby body. As was his habit, he threw his rifle behind his back and cautiously approached the river. Keeping a hunting pace, Poloun came out through the ancient, twisted birch. He had known this place for a long time.

Holding its breath, nature anticipated sunrise, the sky wrapped in an orange shawl. From the damp and silent forest, an autumn scarlet rowan tree and a wrinkled brown alder stared at the dreaming river inlet. They would not admire their fall apparel much longer. Soon the burning frost would sear their leaves; they would stand naked and chilled and tremble all winter in angry winds. From the dense forest pine trees rose. Sullen, reticent, they grumbled and guarded the silence.

On the other bank of the river the lower branches of a rowan tree twitched. A

Nyvkh traditionally had both summer and winter dwellings: a summer house close to fishing grounds and a winter house close to hunting grounds. This is an example of a summer house. Circa 1900.

squirrel pulled at drooping bunches of berries. "It knows when to pick berries— rowan berry is sweetest after a light frost," the old man thought. Summer-orange fur still spotted the squirrel's smoke-colored back. "You're so ugly," the old man smiled. As if embarrassed by being caught looking undignified, the squirrel scampered into the bushes.

Deep in the grove of alder trees and birch shrubs on the other bank of the river, a lonely titmouse twittered persistently. Two pink hazel grouses sat on a naked cherry tree branch over the old man's head. They fell as quiet as fungus-growth. Poloun's soul felt like the surface of a wide inlet during silent weather. A slight wind is enough to cause ripples to run and ruffle the mirror-smooth surface.

Poloun quietly stepped down to the river to refresh his tearing eyes with icy water. From the sky at his feet, up looked an old man with white hair sticking out in every direction. Fright and surprise registered in his wrinkled old larch tree-bark face and in his pale lusterless eyes. His chapped lips remained half opened as if something hard and invisible had stuck in his mouth.

Tif, the Season of the Road, was coming. The old man thought of the soft dents left by sable paws on fresh snow. Soon Poloun would go to the *taiga.* He would set up traps and ask Kurig to be generous. Poloun would ask for black sables only. He was never greedy, even when he fished with a crew. How many fish did they catch? No one could count.

A long time ago, Poloun's ancestors crossed Sakhalin following the *Kongre* (west) wind towards sunrise across the high mountain range, Arkvoval. They came out into a sunny valley, densely crowded with mighty poplars. Fast and icy streams of water united here and turned into a great river. Thousands of salmon spawned in numerous *taiga* stretches. They called the newfound river *Tymi*—spawning river. Poloun's ancestors stayed at the Tymi because it was rich with fish. Nowadays, fish decreased with each year—that worried the old man of the Kevongun tribe.

The Russians taught Nyvkhs to dig the ground and to put potatoes in holes. Many Nyvkhs in the village slowly got

Vladimir M. Sangi

accustomed to agriculture but Poloun remained a fisherman and a hunter. Like other Tymi Nyvkhs, he was reluctant to learn new skills. Only sometimes would he work on his small piece of land. It was always a surprise when he threw a potato in a hole in the beginning of summer and pulled out eighteen in the fall!

The older Poloun got, the more he meditated on his life. Lately, an incomprehensible tenderness towards any living thing grew in him. He stopped burying live puppies in snow. Now, after raising them, he gave them to his neighbors. Let there be more dogs.

During the spawning of salmon he came out to the river before sunrise and sat stooped over the shore for a long time. No one knew what pulled him down there or what occupied his mind;

A Nyvkh family setting out in canoes to visit neighbors. The seal harpoon rests in the Y-shaped device on the gunwale of the canoe. Circa 1900.

he couldn't explain to himself why he came to the spawning ground. Tenderly and sadly he looked at the fish and beams of that characteristic smile that all good souls share spread over his face.

In these times he was burnt by a thought that never left him: *Salmon might come no more!* It lifted him from the bench in his house where he spent most of his time. It pushed him outside where he wandered at loose ends. He was probably not the only one bothered by this thought. Not far from the old Nyvkh settlement Tlavo, Russians were putting together strange buildings. Somebody said that they hatched salmon eggs. Poloun never went there.

That summer, right before the salmon spawning season, the rumor spread through the village like fire in a dry forest: the most ancient Kevong had joined the Fisheries Patrol. It was incomprehensible! Why should a Nyvkh become a Fish Control Inspector? Is it his business what others fish? Nobody prohibits Nyvkhs to fish during *Iukola*. His relatives teased him. "Poloun probably cut up both his nets," they said, sucking on their pipes. But Poloun filled his scorched pipe with rough tobacco, inhaled and pretended not to hear. At first poachers tried everything to cajole the old man, but he hunted them coldly. They began to threaten to catch him somewhere and drown him. Poloun grinned only slightly in response.

Since the new Fisheries Patrol began scaring poachers off, fining them and bringing others to court, the spawning grounds calmed down and Poloun's soul felt more at ease. Even his walk became more buoyant.

This morning he was alert to something. He looked into the water and saw a pair of salmon. Every time Poloun saw fish spawning it transformed him. Even when his spirit was down he found himself squinting into a smile. He enjoyed the thought that he, an ancient Kevong, was guarding salmon offspring from bad people. Poloun walked a little up the river and stopped at a shallow stretch—a spawning ground. It boiled with salmon.

The old man bent over the water. Here was a huge swollen-belly female. Her left fin looked worn out. And the male had a crimson paunch on his side. How long did it take for them to come from the far ocean to Tymi's upper reaches? Nobody knew. All along the way walls of iron hooks, nets in the ocean and predator's teeth waited for them. Many of their brothers and sisters never made it to the furthest grounds but these had managed. Battered and wounded, they reached the place where they had to leave life after themselves.

Poloun felt like petting each fish with his stiff hand. He had enough tenderness for all of them.

The female salmon barely floated, looking for a place to lay her eggs. From one side a long male salmon swam close but the one with the scarred belly grabbed at him with his huge mouth. Like an arrow, the long one stretched up stream. The scarred male returned to his female. Slowly she looked for the proper place. The male hurried her, poked her with his hook nose and tried to bite her. The female slipped away from his sharp teeth.

There she stopped, pressed herself against the pebbles and pumped the bottom with her fins. *She likes this place.* She hit the bottom with her tail. The stream pulled silt like dust. She dug a small hole, stopped and froze in place, her tail quivering nervously. And then the golden thread streamed into the hole! There were hundreds of eggs and the sun played in each of them. The water was saturated with resilient sunlight—the fish swimming in the sun.

Poloun's heart trembled—he could see the beginning of life! Here they were, thousands of future salmon! The male curled around impatiently, opening his mouth, warning and threatening other males. Finally, the female wagged her tail listlessly and moved aside. The

Vladimir M. Sangi

male rapidly took her position. White and murky clouds covered the sparkling eggs. Then the male began to hit the bottom with his tail, carefully hiding the hole, the cradle of his offspring.

All around, hundreds of similar pairs committed this act of continuing their kind. Afterwards, they floated over the hills of pebbles, guarding them, falling apart and dying. The stream carried their flaccid bodies to shore.

Poloun backed up, quietly moved away from the spawning ground and headed further up. A kilometer from here was another spawning ground. How are things going there?

From far away, his experienced ear caught the sounds of splashing water. Who was that? A bear? Poloun loaded his rifle. Fast but soft steps brought him to the bushes at the river's edge. He looked out cautiously.

A man in high rubber boots was standing in the water. Deftly, he hit salmon with a spear and threw them on the shore. There were a few dozen fish already lying there. Some of them had their bellies slit. Nearby stood a barrel.

"He's stocking eggs,"—this thought pierced Poloun's heart.

The man threw a spear into the fish floating by and lifted it trembling over the water. From a wound sparkling with bleeding tears, elastic eggs streamed down into the water.

Poloun recognized the poacher as Serioga, who once lived on the Tymi River. The man had been recruited to Sakhalin as a tractor driver. From Nyvkhs he learned how to salt salmon eggs. During the day Serioga worked in the field and at night he fished salmon and sold his game.

Poloun had already experienced an unpleasant stand-off with him. Last fall the old hunter was coming back from inspecting his area, and at this very spawning ground he unexpectedly ran into Serioga, who was stocking caviar the same way he did now. That time Serioga gave him a glass of vodka and made him promise not to tell anyone.

Feeling somebody staring at him Serioga suddenly turned around with fear in his eyes. He saw a stranger standing behind leaning on a rifle. His fear vanished in recognition and his eyes began to shine. "Ah, that is you, Poloun! Why are you staring at me?" Poloun didn't move and Serioga stopped smiling. Holding his attention, the poacher slowly came to shore.

"Come over here," Serioga's voice broke. Poloun did not move. "Come on, come over here, come to me! Morning is cold . . . but I have something to warm

Nyvkh hunters with spears preparing for a bear hunt, a ritualized and sacred event. Circa 1900.

us up." The poacher smiled rapaciously and put his long knife covered with salmon blood in front of him.

"Here's what," Poloun spoke carefully. "Get out of here! And don't think of coming back! If I see you stepping on this ground, I will kill you! I will track you like a bear and kill you. No thieves get away from me. Leave!"

That was the last case of poachers that year. It became quiet at every spawning ground.

When the spawning season ended, Poloun's relatives couldn't recognize the old Kevong. He became sociable. He visited his neighbors. Poloun looked younger and even his back straightened. It seemed like his gnawing thoughts were forgotten.

❖

The Season of the Road passed. Winter stepped into its rights. Many hunters had already turned in their fur. Poloun had just finished his preparations for hunting. He wanted to hurry to the *taiga!* There, ancient centuries-old pine trees with snow collars withstand the strong winds which scarcely penetrate the dense forest. There, cautious sables leave soft paw prints on the fresh snow.

The old man's wide, flexible hunter's skis with ringed seal fur on the bottoms slid easily over the crumbly snow. Poloun came to a large lake, connected to the Tymi River by a channel. To avoid a long detour, the hunter decided to cross the lake. He took his skis off, tied them with a rope and dragged them behind. At the shore frozen water formed several layers of ice. Further out the ice was clear. One could see islands of algae on the yellow bottom.

Suddenly something wiggled under the ice. It was alive and frightening. A tremor ran through Poloun's body. His hair reared and lifted his hat. Who was that, moving at the bottom like a shadow? Was it a water ghost who watched for him? The old man squinted his little round eyes intensely in an effort to see who was there.

Large and dark, it came closer and closer. Soon it gained the shape of a fish.

Vladimir M. Sangi

Two Nyvkh women
in traditional dress.
Circa 1900.

It was a huge hunchback male salmon with crimson-brown stripes on his sides. Slowly, in deep meditation, he floated right under the old man's feet. Poloun bent down on his knees and began to examine the fish.

Strange! All the salmon finished laying eggs a long time ago and died. But this one was alive. His scarred sides were evidence of a difficult route from the ocean to the upper reaches of the river. His gills had faded, worn out. Like a shaggy beard, green algae clung to them.

"Salmon didn't shoot his milt," the old man thought. "He didn't leave offspring after him, and *Kowrne* punished him with a long and lonely useless life. And with his scary look he will startle the other fish of the lake."

Poloun felt sorry for the salmon. He would stop this poor fish from suffering. But how to do it? There was a thick layer of ice between the man and the fish. The old man's eyes clouded; all his life he lived alone.

"So why have you remained unmarried?" the old man asked the salmon.

The motionless eyes of the fish refracted through water and ice, growing bigger and bigger. Now the old man clearly saw the two huge fish eyes and in them—a ghostly reproach.

(Translated from Russian.)

VLADIMIR M. SANGI (Nyvkh) is considered the founder of Nyvkh written literature. He has transcribed the Nyvkh alphabet and is the author of a Nyvkh language manual as well as a recipient of the State Prize of the Russian Federation.

Mr. Sangi was born in 1935 in the Nogliki District of Sakhalin. He began his studies at a local school for Nyvkh children but continued on at the Hertzen Pedagogical University in Saint Petersburg. There he began to publish poetry and short stories in magazines. After graduation he returned to Sakhalin to teach at the Nyvkh school and was appointed Minorities Affairs Inspector for Nogliki District Committee. In that capacity he visited remote settlements, meeting with Nyvkhs, Oroks, Evenks and Nanais, all Siberian ethnic tribes. He began to write traditional Nyvkh stories creating the body of his first book, *Nyvkh Legends*, published in 1961. The book was nationally acknowledged and the chairman of the USSR Writers' Union wrote in response, "The first Nyvkh writer has appeared. He came to open the soul and the heart of his people to others."

Many books followed. Most explore Sangi's main theme, that of the relationship between humans and nature. He writes about courage and honor, about the human place in life, about the blood ties of humans with their native land. He is widely known for his novels, short stories, fairy tales and essays. The "New Books of Sovremennik" series included Sangi's epic *Human of Ykh-Myth*, written after ancient tales. Sangi also compiled a folklore collection of twenty-six tribes of the Russian North and initiated a series of books by tribal authors.

He has received many awards and honors, including the title Secretary of the Writers' Union of Russia, and was awarded "The Sign of Honor." He lived and wrote in Moscow between 1974 and 1996 then returned to the Nogliki settlement on Sakhalin. There he continues to write and to advocate for the Nyvkh and Orok people and their way of life.

Vladimir M. Sangi

Lee Maracle

Where Love Winds Itself Around Desire

Raven can do anything.

Inspired, she can gather the spirit world together, engaging everything—flora, fauna, stone, wind and sea—in a single decision-making process. She is powerful, clever and tricky. She can re-create sound and transform you, engage you in a way you have never been engaged. Not too long ago she gathered sound from the earth's air waves, shrunk them into tiny balls, wrapped them in rain drops, carried them to the sea and dropped them where we swam. I knew she would follow me, nagging and harassing me with sound until she got the response she wanted, so naturally I swallowed the balls of sound, translated them into my own language and agreed to return my response to the world.

Raven is nosy—in a good way.

She's always minding the business of the rest of the world, eavesdropping, weighing voice and action against consequence. She minds the business of the two-leggeds the most. They're all a bunch of loose cannons. Humans are capable of wanting things which defy their needs, counter their interests and destroy the very spiritual sensibility they were given when they came into the world. The original humans of Turtle Island were there in the sky world when we all received our original instructions. We were there. Does anyone remember? It seems to me that it is incumbent on the original humans to share this piece of vital information. Oh well, who am I to judge, you are returning to the same place you came from and your grandmothers all eagerly await your return—they still remember how to deal with you. The only responsibility I have right now is to talk to you.

"The Canadian people must protect their salmon stocks from U.S. incursion."

It is a spiritual world. Spirit moves living beings like wind moves weather. The why of it doesn't matter to us. We just accept that this is the way things happen. Hidden inside Spirit are our intentions, our original desire, and from there is born character.

All original characters existed in the sky world before we took on physical form. We were all instructed to be careful of one another, interact with one another, gauge consequence of our actions and return to the sky wiser than when we came. From this body of wisdom comes the laws governing conduct. Our desire is tempered by the laws handed down to us from our ancestors. Minnows know not to tangle with barracuda. It is a law which was handed to us to govern our conduct. It is also rooted in a piece of wisdom. We have no desire to live outside our wisdom. Our sense of desire is rooted in the belief that we must learn to find the freedom to fulfill desire within the ancient context of wisdom we inherit.

Desire is wonderment. Want is desire. Desire arises from the pure place of light inside the body. Light, fire and spirit hothouse desire. Life can twist desire, shrink it, shrivel it, drown it until there is little fire left. This happened to us many generations ago. We stopped doing the things we were doing because this shrinking of our fire didn't feel good. We too thought we wanted the freedom to do just as we pleased. There are consequences for that. Some humans can barely move on behalf of themselves. They have become so twisted they will hurt one another in the name

of desire. They have hurt so many of my relatives in the name of desire.

We have agreements between us and the sea, between us and the children of the sea and between us and the humans. We uphold these agreements. We seek freedom within the limits established by these agreements. The humans we have agreements with know who we are and we recognize them. We are not anyone's "fishing stock." We have no agreement with the new humans. There is a way to make this agreement—a spiritual way. The original humans know how to do this, but first they must come together with the new humans, make an agreement between themselves, then make one with us.

Sometimes I feel for Raven. I know she's been talking to humans, some have even been listening, but they have a strange assortment of power authorities with tin ears. Maybe they have slippery brains. Anyway the sound went out, some people picked it up, talked to the other humans who didn't believe them.

Once the humans on this coast operated on belief—in one another, in us, in all living beings—even stone, air, fire and water were considered part of the living beings who were worthy of sharing belief.

In the memory of my body is a time when all the humans on the island listened to one another in a believing way. When someone heard Raven sing, no one questioned it. They would talk over the song, decipher what it meant, determine what they had to change, and change. It was all so simple. But now, different humans people the island and something has happened to the descendants of the original ones. Some of the great-grandchildren of humans don't sound at all like their forefathers. The language is different and the way they hear and respond is different. Some of them still hear Raven and attempt to do her bidding, but they run into problems with other humans. It is all such a. . . . Oh well, I am judging and that is not my place. I just know that Raven would not be singing to me if she had received the human response she wanted.

I don't have much time. I failed to master the landscape of your story; its structure eludes me, slips through the sounds reaching my ears, touching chords you do not possess. I own feelings, I am Spirit, I have no language with which to fuss over presentation, but I do know about response. Here are the words I heard from the rain drops Raven gave me. This is my response.

"Despite all the studies conducted by the federal government, the journey of the salmon continues to be a mystery."

I knew from the moment my tiny body freed itself from my mother's home I would make this journey. The sun hit the silver bank near the river's edge where the imagination lives. It shot warm heat through water as our many numbers nudged, bumped and scrambled for a place in the crook of the river bank where Momma had built our mud home. It was shallow, crowded and slightly noisy. We barely had time to recognize each other, identify the family markings separating us from other minnows, before we all headed out to sea.

From this place of the imagination are born our images of the journey ahead. The enthusiasm for the open sea swells inside, pricking at the feeling of trepidation, drowning it with the prospect of excitement. It happens a moment at a time. Image after image of the river is shown to us; the excitement inside is swallowed. The downstream swim is illuminated and met with eager anticipation. As the old light of previous ancestral swims shines on the images inside, the courage to try is coded into the very blood of my body. The burbling sound of so many of us brings up a mix of melancholy and wonderment. The awesomeness of all of us having come from the same couple, the very knowing that both of them killed

Lee Maracle

themselves for this moment, is humbling. They did so knowing they would never see us all together like this, scrambling for the sea, jiggling inside, enthusiasm for the journey battling the twinges of fear of the open sea. They died knowing most of us would not make it. They left behind this amazing steel thread of willingness to try.

". . . the journey continues to be a mystery."

I know from the moment we begin, most of us won't return. I look at each one of us. I have to. It goes against all my logical smarts to look at as many of my siblings as I can, commit them to memory, but the looking is not about logic. It is the only time I will see us all together like this. They look like me, scared, excited, knowing the end as well as the beginning, and committed, committed to the greatest swim, this journey against the very direction of the sea, the river and the rain. To make this journey we must buck the roil of the tide, its storm swells pushing up our will, fan our own fire inside and strengthen our musculature. The very massage of cold sea against hot muscle births awesome desire: desire for victory, desire for challenge, desire for procreation so big we will take on the sea. Minnows are the only sea children who are capable

and committed enough to take on natural power.

We all know what will inspire us to do so, too. Passion. Romance, my Meer'ah. Sleek, spirited, elegant Meer'ah. I had no idea when I would make the connection with her, but I knew I would. In the moments before I left, my imagination called her up, dreamt her, imaged up her being that I might recognize her even through the dark layers of the sea.

I know this river, every eddy, every safe spot, rest area, fall, rapid and cold spot. I know where the sun always rests its warming light. I know where River captures log and debris in dangerous tangled webs of deadwood about to explode. I know where the water lies too still, becomes stagnant, bottom-weighted with things not meant to live there. Things you name cadmium, mercury, aluminum, tailings, waste, garbage, toxic chemicals. We have no name for them, we just know to avoid those places at all costs; filtering such water through our gills weakens the body. I know I require a strong body.

Minnows are born knowing they are capable of living outside of motherhood. From birth I challenged this river, then I headed for the open sea to take it on. We are born with our eyes open, our minds sharp, our consciousness formed, our journey set. By the time the journey downstream is complete, the map to our sector of the ocean is already clear.

There is no quarreling with ourselves about direction, destiny or duty. We find our freedom within the context we were handed with grace and dignity. It is how we are *siem* (in the spirit of everything).

"*. . . despite government studies, the journey . . .*"

I am not sure that you can discover anything when you've already made some pretty big decisions about the thing you're studying. The notion that we have no brain and no heart is one of the stupidest declarations those above us have made. Fish can't think, their brains don't function in the same way. It doesn't occur to any of these heroes that our brains don't function like theirs because we are less confused. We are incapable of confusion. It doesn't dawn on them that perhaps this may not be a measure of our thoughtless stupidity, but rather a measure of our capacity for single-minded thoughtfulness.

"*. . . is a mystery.*"

I know enough about creatures everywhere on sea, land, in the air to know not to make intimate pronouncements about them. We know it makes no sense to believe we are capable of jumping outside ourselves to really see from someone else's perspective. Our journey is about life, spirit, passion and respect. We believe we share this with every creature, every stone, every water drop, even sun, moon and stars.

Because we cannot see outside of our own perspective we are careful to hold fast to the principles above. Outside of Raven magic, we share no common language, which makes for huge communication mishaps. If I don't take this opportunity, then no communication is possible at all. I know this is the only moment I have to comment on what I hear and see about the humans and I seize it. I don't mind seeming unfair or stupid.

The humans up above who fail to understand why it is we would knock ourselves out for love must have a very shallow definition for it. I hear them say good words like " 'til death do us part," but it isn't how they live. "I'll be good to you as long as you are perfect for me" seems more like it. From a minnow's perspective this is shallow, which is probably appropriate since humans cannot swim in deep water. Deep thinking, deep feeling, the very treacherousness of the journey through life until death do you

Lee Maracle

part is understood by minnows. Humans don't seem to love very deeply at all. Our affection, our betrothal to our spouses, our progeny is incomprehensible to humans.

". . . a mystery."

The very moment two particles are called into being, wind is born, creating movement between the two. This movement is forever an elemental ceremony of attraction, gentled and tethered by odd moments of repulsion, rejoined by attraction and calmed by kinetic rest. Kinetic rest is magic. At rest, power is accumulated. Energy born becomes willful, spirited and desirous of re-attraction. Desire is ever romantic for beings whose veins pump red-hot life, fluid life, blood life. The spirit of desire inside the blood creates the yearning to move, to arc across the universe to touch each being in some place where origin is awakened, memoried and cherished. Wind and breath against being creates sound, the medium of exchange between beings. Sound. *Breath tracks** of original movement, the expression of emotive being, the appeal to desire is forever. It rides wind, trips among trees, skims across water surface, plunges through deep water, is amplified by hurricanes of windsong, is seized by living bodies who have not forgotten they exist only

to carry Spirit, push up the arc of light and express ancient timeless emotion.

Love. Midnight's dreamspace. Love. The body's electric message. Love. The mind's preoccupation. Love. Breath's destiny. Love. The body's craving. Love our swansong, wind's caress, skin's sentient being, the reckoning between beings, the spark igniting the fire within, the power source of light's arc. We commit to memory all that has come before us. In our bodies lies the memory of all time, the remembering of our love, our parents' love, our ancestors' love. The few who survived loved so deeply, so completely, that they were granted the gift of future progeny.

These people who call our love a mystery stretch their insolence beyond imagination. To live outside of imagination is to refuse to picture the self in its most glorious being. To live on the periphery of the imagined fullness of self is to hide within the shell of your own being, unable to see beyond. To hide within yourself is to narrow the field of vision the earth and all her children offer up. To narrow the field of vision of earth is to blind yourself to the power of spiritual seeing.

At first, it didn't matter. The battle for the fruit of the sea hadn't heated up until recently. Besides, I was just a little fry when I first heard the voices. Sun

*Breath tracks, coined by Jeannette C. Armstrong to describe writing, and twisted by Lee Maracle to mean remembered words.

Lee Maracle performing a blessing on the dry stones of the Squamish River.

lightning joins the fracas. Those moments are special for us. Lightning cuts jagged shafts through all those layers of green, sparking up amazing activity from the deep. Puffer fishes swell, eels seek the shafts of light, jelly fishes throb, even Meer'ah and I get excited.

Once, just once, a shaft of bent light caught her at just the right angle, her body curved—moon-crescent silver shining alone in the sea of dark. A gentle halo of light backdropped the curve of her frame.

Magic. The sea, the wind, lightning and the two-leggeds' grandfather thunderers can make magic. It charges you up to be tossed and turned in the power of the earth's older and more mature children playing and having a real bust-'em-up good time. A celebration so wild, so powerful, it stops the breath of all but stone.

Barracudas hide during such times. They aren't particularly social and I've never known them to be too friendly. Sharks watch from the giant kelp grounds, looking like they aren't sure just how they should react. Me and Meer'ah like riding the great waves of the sea during such gatherings, trying hard to embrace all that power, feel it, internalize it.

At such times the two-leggeds above us holler out across all those electrical

danced across the tips of the water folds chasing one another to the sea. The brook widened, I slid over the falls, just before my home stream joins another river. The voices came out of nowhere. I wasn't sure then, what carried them, now I know. Wind and water play with sound. It's their toy. They spend their entire lives catching voice, tossing it about, juggling the sounds, racing through the trees and singing out when they like what they hear. When the thunderers—the grandfathers of the original two-legged get to gabbing— wind, rain and water sing. Sometimes

Lee Maracle

lines, "Gale warning . . . hurricane alert . . . storm warnings . . . stay off the sea . . ." and such. Those on the sea scurry to return to port. Those on shore scurry to batten down the hatches, return to safe houses, much like barracudas looking for a cave.

There is an uncanny connection between two-leggeds, sharks and barracudas. I know the original humans know what I am talking about, but I don't think anyone else has heard this story. Barracuda has a winning grin and sharks, when they're panicked, go right into a feeding frenzy. It seems that all a hungry barracuda has to do is figure how to send them into this frenzy, then clean up the leftovers. It's what they do. Don't get me wrong, I'm not passing judgment on being a barracuda. It's OK to be one, but you've got to be prepared to live alone. It's how they are *siem*.

There is a species of two-leggeds up there that behaves much the same way, mostly men, and although I have never seen any of them, I have heard them. They talk through their noses in high-pitched, stretched-out, strident voices like they are in chronic pain. Hollering like their ears don't work so well. They sound half-angry almost all the time, even their laughter sounds sinister.

Sound. It's what I know. In my world of water, sound is amplified, nuance is so easily readable. Sound has texture, tone, rhythm and meaning quite apart from the words being uttered. In its amplification, sound tells its own story. Underneath the rhythm, the tone speaks to emotion, addresses the spirit, invites response. When the two-legged sharks and barracudas speak, they invite cannibalism or isolation. Their words are either door-closers to oneness or openers to madness: barracudas wait, ever ready to make the feeding frenzy happen. Sharks are wary, know what each other is capable of and watch each other suspiciously. There is nothing wrong with being a shark as long as you're willing to "stand on guard" forever. It's how they are *siem*. Barracudas only need to seize the opportunity to engineer it all.

> "Scientists are unable to determine how it is these sockeye know which particular river of the some 1800 rivers and streams on the West Coast . . ."

Now there's a piece of arrogance. They're surprised we remember our birthplace. Can't figure out how it is we come to remember home. We aren't like them, moving every six months, having one child in Boston, moving to L.A. to have another and finally settling in Seattle. Are they daft? How do they know from the rows and rows of houses which one is theirs? I swear some of them must have to memorize their own address to find their home.

I'm genuinely puzzled about whether or not their eyes work. I wonder if they even look at the rivers inundating the coast line, each one unique, different from the last. My river's opening is U-shaped like the carved u's on the welcome poles of the original humans. The dark color of the water against the land forms the wings of the graceful U. Its U-wedge is slate gray against the warm pale green. When the sun shines on it, it takes on a baby blue hue, transforming the pastel green into a pretty turquoise jewel. Just inside the outline of the U there are four stones marking the entrance. Great round stones. The first has an image of *Tsuniguid* etched into the stone to remind us of the beauty of deep thought, darkness and the peace inherent in recognition of truth beyond the shallow edges of the sea. The second stone is bumpy and patched with green and black lichen. She speaks to the memory of food and the journey of swallowing life's pleasures. The third stone wears a skirt of mussels, shake-dancing through storm after storm. Their song signals our welcome and good speed home. The song sings congratulations on the completion of our first journey out to sea, our second journey of surviving the sea and our third journey to the mouth of the river which will be our last. The last stone is smooth —our prayer stone, wishing us good speed, successful journey.

". . . the mystery of why it is these fish will scale falls, leap over and over again, crashing on sharp stones, continuing to leap until they scale the falls or die trying is unknown after a half century of marine study . . ."

Hello, up there.

If you could see my Meer'ah, light twinkling against clear pearled scales, skin slate gray with the slightest hint of midnight blue peering through, the whiteness of her smooth belly marking the entrance to her womanhood. Look at her, belly bulging with young. Watch her, leaping, heavy with child, swimming with strong determination for home. See the way her body twists through crashing waves, between rocks, the agility, the grace, feel her vulnerability and witness her tenacious will, you'd not wonder at her at all. If you knew the woman you loved would wait for you in that silver space between river and bank, wait until you arrived or die waiting, you'd know why I leap, uttering my own encouragement, leap, utter some more and leap until I make the falls or die trying.

In a sea storm her body sings, water whistling through her scales. She dives

Lee Maracle

for kelp, eyes not looking left or right, just straight down at the tips of the giant, jelly-soft sea grass, waving at us. Inside the haven of kelp the water plays with plant, murmuring sounds of soothing softness to both of us. Delicate strands of kelp swaying sensuously, touching, dancing, playing with our bodies, reaching deep inside to that sacred place of being where love winds itself around desire and touch rekindles the fire of passion.

This passion wraps itself around our memory from first fish to now. We remember every struggle to return home. We return to the same home, generation after generation. Memory after memory of every trip, the markers, the stones, the eddies, the falls are all known to us from birth. We are not disconnected from our bodies, our lineage memory, our spirits, all work together to instruct us, compel us to return home. Home holds powerful sweetness for us. The scent of it, the feel of it, conjures well-being, future and eternal life through birth, re-birth and common songs of life between us.

We came to the sea by the falls, past rock and through the deadwood debris River owns and collects as playmates. The familiarity of it, the knowing we may not survive it, the challenge it awakens inside to move through all the obstacles, is seductive. It addresses deep need inside us to rise to the occasion. To struggle with ourselves and win. We do not view stone as an enemy but respect the spirit inside. The voices we hear when we "crash against rock" are old voices, our voices, they stay inside the stone and echo words of self-encouragement to those who come later. To crash against Stone is to be honored with our own opportunity to whisper self-encouraging words and add our voices to the voices of our ancestors before us. Without Stone's sharp edges we could not know the depth of softness. Without Stone's guardianship there would be no one to cradle the words of encouragement to the next generation. We acknowledge and respect our agreement with Stone.

"Environmentalists' conference shows threatened salmon stocks and makes a case for more closures on the open sea."

I repeat, we have an agreement between us and the original humans. Don't think for a minute that closing or opening fishing sites is going to obviate the necessity for the new humans, from which environmentalists spring, to enter into an agreement with us too. Don't think for a moment that you as humans have an earthly right to determine how many of us will or will not sacrifice our lives for your survival. Don't imagine we ever gave any being the authority to act on our behalf.

I wonder if maybe the environmentalists aren't the most ridiculous humans of all. They cite our demise as the basis for fishing closures as though there were no spirit-place for us beyond our mortal beginnings. As though we weren't dead-sure of death at the end of birth. We are aware of the remarkability of survival. We know how many brothers and sisters we have at the moment of birth, we also know how few return to this, our spawning ground. Most of our life is about death, living with it, surrounded by it, under constant threat of it. Death portends not terror, not sadness but release, eternal freedom and peace.

It is not death that is the problem here. It is the absence of permission to engage us which continues to threaten you. Without our permission you will sicken. Without our permission you are violating the spirit of another being. It is the rape of the spirit of Sockeye which will haunt you not just in this world but in the sky world after you leave here. Eternity is not finished with you yet.

The issue becomes complicated when environmentalists get hold of a cause. It is not enough to simply say—we are tampering with Sockeye's playground without permission. You need to find a way to secure Sockeye's agreement and express our gratitude for Salmon's existence, you need to be careful not to commit Sockeye to the joy of death in a senseless and wasteful fashion. Your life holds promise based on how you conduct yourself. You need to remember that your current conduct holds promise: it promises to bring you trouble. We seriously *are* living beings. We *require* your respect for our perfect right to be before we will cooperate with you.

Humans behave as though they are unaware that this is our playground, this great water resort was intended for our use. It seems huge to the two-legged barracudas above us. When you look to the depths of my watery playground and don't see its finiteness, don't see me and my need for its breadth or its depth, you are bound to make ridiculous pronouncements. No one up there feels the power, the strength or the fragility of the metric tons of salty water it takes to procreate the life below. We are all just so much potential harvest or cause for protection as powerless victims.

The sea has character, moves in accordance with its own personality, is driven by its own rhythm. She rolls, folds, rises and falls to her own private power song. This movement makes it possible for everyone to survive. Hurricanes are her desperate attempts

Lee Maracle

Shannon Falls, north of Vancouver, B.C. Coastal Salish people tell of the double-headed sea serpent who created the Falls.

and their scientists build equipment, conduct research that gives them a huge capacity to "harvest us" without challenge, without permission.

Some harvest. My home, my relatives have all been reduced to a giant flea market for the men above.

❧

I want you to know who I am. Before I die I want someone up there to see me, to see my lady of the sea. I want you to follow me, to hear me and feel for me as I journey from here to home.

I was born a thousand miles from where I live. I play between the mouth of the stream that emptied onto the sea and here. I will need the thousand miles of space to flex and build the muscle it will take to make my final journey home. For the next four years I will focus on playing, gamboling, leaping waves, riding currents, familiarizing myself with the very nature of water, all in readiness for my last great splash. Daily, I challenge myself until I return with my sweetheart for our last great moment together: the birth of our progeny.

Water amplifies sound. We can hear you up there, your voices trickle down, sometimes in a hodge-podge of unreadable sound. Occasionally I catch a clear set of words, nasal sounding,

to spread the food around for the larger life to eat. We, who live here, know how to ride them, hide from them, sense the water's warnings and ready ourselves to survive them. Cold caps mean cold weather, slow down, rest, reflect, winter is here. Smooth water means play. Humans don't seem to take note of what is happening to us down below. It is a terrible thing to study life from your own agenda. They tag my relatives, watch their journey so they can know where we are when the hunt is on. Those men in boats above once had to read the sea, watch us, speculate on our whereabouts. Now their government bubbling out: "Roger, I'm at Millbank Sound. Over." I presume it is some enemy of mine trying to plan a joint assault with buddies of his species. I pay no attention.

My sweetheart, she's there, the sun barely breaking through the layers of deep ocean green, hinting light against her slender silver body. She's resting in the only sun ray hereabouts. You can't see her but I want you to know what she looks like, so I will tell you in language you understand.

All in all she is just under nine pounds, four inches high at her center, seventeen inches long altogether. Her scales shine silver white under the clear green and in moments when the sun squeezes through all the dark the ocean's depth spawns, she almost blinks. The water passes over her gills with such elegance you can't hear her even under the sea. She is a powerful swimmer, flipping her tail fins, her dorsal and side fins with grace and strength. When I watch her in our interminable search for food, I get so caught up sometimes that I wish the day of reckoning was upon us, sweet love.

I know her. I have nuzzled every scale, slid gently to her side during sea storms when the water is churning out fifteen-foot waves. I have sensed barracudas coming into our home waters,

dived to the sea floor, hidden in the kelp with her, until danger passed. I know how she shakes after danger is over. Her little thin body quivers so prettily, it sparks so much emotion in me that if I were *skana* I would weep. I know what it feels like to love someone so deeply you are prepared to die for her. You don't. You're human.

What you-all don't know is that you are capable of this love, but you must travel for a long time to get there. I remember once people who used to talk to us. They stood by the sea for days and days, asking where we were, storying up their need for us, numbering the need. We didn't mind those people. They took days to finish all the hullaballoo they put into their request: *ceremony*, they say in the language of the newcomers. Some of these people still believe we required all that pomp and hoopla. In a strange sort of way it is true.

Because it took days for them to ask, we all had a chance to get together and decide who would be sacrificed. We named those who would be pulled from the weirs and speared for consumption. The women who managed the catch listened to us, really looked at us, saw the spirit of sacrifice on our bodies, read the sound of agreement and speared and netted those we had selected. We know who to send to hold up our agreement.

Lee Maracle

We know the sheen our bodies have to emanate to catch the attention of the original fishers. We have always been willing to hold up our end of the bargain and don't need the ceremony for that. We do need the time to determine who among us shall express our desire that your life shall be honored by our death.

Those people who have agreements with us have descendants though they seem to lack power. The new humans don't believe the old, don't hear them and don't feel the need to engage us in any kind of deals whatsoever. If it can't wheel and deal in cash, these new humans can't understand it. Get the coins out of your ears and the jing of the cash registers out of your minds. Your deafness arises out of the coin-jingling din of profit and loss filling up the spaces where your brain ought to be.

Pay attention. Attention is the only debt you owe the natural world. Pay attention. We talk. We breathe, we love, we live and we know a little about our own life and love. Pay Attention. It is the only debt that is dangerous to ignore.

"Violence heats up in the salmon wars . . ."

Oh please. We are not at war. We have no way of going to war. We have no memory of how to participate in such a fiasco. This is your war. You are fighting over one another. You are fighting one another for the right to possess, defile and violate other beings. War is often like that.

It is not a *salmon* war. It is a man war. Men are at war. It is not about Salmon either. Since we have no agreement with most of you to provide your bodies with food, and since most of you catch us, sell us and receive money in exchange for our dead bodies, it is not about Salmon at all. You are at war over who gets the most money. We have seen what you do with your money.

Your homes are chock-full of expensive toys. Long ago you gave up singing. Without song, humans like any other being, will die. When you gave up singing you engaged other humans to sing in your place. More humans were engaged in designing electric toys which would carry their songs into your homes.

Learn to sing. Give up your toys. Save yourself from a fate far worse then death—an empty life.

Think. Pay attention. Without song, your desire has no doorway from which to enter your spirit. Without desire, your body has no way to experience emotions. Without emotion, you have no way to enjoy love. Without love, you have no need for your eyes. To truly see, your eyes need to be able to feast on the beauty of life. Without seeing you cannot hear. Your ears respond to the feast life presents.

"Threatened salmon stocks . . ."

We are not under threat. You are. You are in danger of living a life of empty numbers governed by equations. Standards and norms run around your brain, racketeering about, looking for another cash register to tally profits instead of losses. Your words are focused toward this end so stubbornly that you cannot conceive of a tear drop of Raven's voice plunking itself into the sea, bringing me your language, your words. You cannot image up my swallowing it. My body played with your sound the way humans should be playing with one another, returned these words to you.

"leap over and over again . . ."

Play with one another. Gather them up. Hold them up to that inner light we know even you new humans possess. In the light, explore the jewel another's thoughts present. Toss these words about inside the musculature of your own sensual being. Feel them in your throat. Let them speak to you. Let them springboard from their origin here at the bottom of the sea, up the rivers, across the swells of ocean. Let this inner light inside you respond in its own way. Free your body of its prison of numbness and let it feel a response. Search only for the words after mine have had a chance to play with you and your body.

". . . continue to leap until they scale the falls"

Come. Play with me. See the pale green waters turn steel slate gray and wonder at the origin of color in the sea. Play with me. See my Meer'ah, her ever so slightly pinkened scales as she catches my eye. See her, the bravery of self-challenge enlivens her. Watch us together as we race for home.

Look at me. This manfish. See me scale the falls. See my body swim with fierce determination. Catch my joy as I leap. Leap for life. Leap for creation. Leap for love. Is there anything else worthy of living for?

Listen to the song Raven sings for you.

Listen to the prayers we all send you.

We are in no danger. Our passing out-of-being is but a moment in time. We will live forever in the spirit world. The recounting of our generations, those who made the swim and those

Lee Maracle

who did not will forever entertain us. We will share the laughter and the spiritual joy of our love, re-watch in our imagination the journey of our children in their infinite numbers as they gather, look about at one another, feel the power of their enthusiasm for the great swim ahead push out their fear, shrink and dissipate it, pushing it outside of their bodies. We will re-look as the multitudes shrink to a few with pride and joy till time closes forever on the earth and still we will re-live these moments our memories hold dear.

"... scale the falls"

You are frail. Acknowledge your fragility. In doing so you will see your strength. Inside of you lives the desire for mortal being. It was placed there long ago for a reason. It was placed there instead of the musculature, the ferocity, others of us naturally possess. It is there in exchange for the huge numbers we were given during the birthing process. It is a fair trade only if you acknowledge you are weak with a powerful desire to hold fast to physical being.

To see it you must first acknowledge your only mother, the earth. That the sea is part of this woman you have yet to hold dear. That we are all family, we are alive, and no being is without con-

sciousness. Even Stone is careful what sounds she holds to her breast to be repeated to those who can hear for all time. Stones don't collect the sounds of cash registers. Stone knows what sounds are worthy of saving and carries out its duties well.

Cedar feels every emotion worthy of your expression. Trees help you to grow those emotions up, respond with grace and dignity to the emotional invitations others extend. Cedar can't respond to nattering and drivel, to whining and complaining. She only responds to those beings whose hearts are clear and whose emotions are pure, without traps. She knows her instructions well and she holds fast to the agreements the original humans made with her. These agreements between us are for your benefit, not mine.

The earth is your mother. Know this. Swallow it. She will spank you if you don't mind. If you run amok, she has ways of recovering. You cannot threaten others, only yourselves. You are the only beings with the sort of tricky consciousness that Raven needs to understand and sing to.

You are wearing Raven out. She, too, has her limits. Pay attention. You can't possibly be so broke that you can't pay attention. She is not calling to you anymore. You don't want her tattling to your mother about your inability to listen.

The sadness in my passing will not be the absence of physical life for me, but rather, the hardship in feeding yourself. You will know hunger again. You know hunger exists elsewhere. You know the depths of despair to which it drives humans. You will know it in your heart soon.

". . . journey still a mystery . . ."

Humans are strange to us down here. We hear you above us, screaming high-pitched desperation between you. The sounds of it full of death for us, death to us, death between us, death around us, all in the name of yourselves. Life. It doesn't work that way, not even for the snow flea on a glacier. No life is conjured by two individuals fighting over the bodies of another individual.

You imagine yourself to be something other than what you are, your parameters have been stretched beyond any reasonable boundaries. I hear the sounds "American, then Canadian then Japanese" as though these names made a difference to who you are and who we are. You all relate to maps in some strange deep way. Boundaries, geography, offshore limits, stretching truth between you beyond all recognition, turns you away from your own goal.

" Salmon wars heat up . . ."

Misnomer seems to be your specialty. You make it sound as though we were at war with one another. We cannot conceive of gathering weapons, teaming up with barracudas and sharks over the bodies and fate of anemones or eels or any other creature. We certainly could not justify rationalizing this, then shouting it out to the world as anything but a war against yourselves.

My body does not belong to you, Canada, U.S. fisher people or consumer. My body belongs to me, to my progeny, to my Meer'ah.

"Canadians seize American boats . . ."

You see. The prize is your tool for harvesting my body. But it is between you-all that the war rages. One of you aggresses, the other defends. Men who never will enter the fight plan and decide its direction. Whole armies will gather weapons, generals will assemble plans; presidents, prime ministers will utter comments that millions will believe and obey—the sharks are about to go into the feeding frenzy. What little is left over after the bloodletting will be divided among those who were clever enough to get others to do the fighting for them—the two-legged barracudas who sit back, smile and wait.

Lee Maracle

We understand Raven. She never gives up. You have no idea what tenacious will, what stubbornness Raven possesses. Be wary. Raven has agreements with the sea. Raven will keep them. She has ways to wake you up. For Raven, change is necessary if things are off track. Change does not have to be good, it only has to be different. We know she's partnering up with Earth and Sea, storming about, cleaning house, altering Life as we know it. Raven is trying desperately to remove the garbage humans have strewn everywhere. Our common mother is helping her. They require your cooperation. Don't keep pushing your luck.

Trust me. You do not want to piss Raven off.

LEE MARACLE (Métis/Coastal Salish) has been in the forefront of the Indian Movement for many years. She has delivered over a thousand speeches on political, historical, feminist and sociological topics related to Native people, conducted over one hundred workshops on personal and cultural reclamation, writing and health through diet. She is a Salish weaver and does traditional Native beadwork. She has also taught at the University of Toronto and Victoria University.

Her published work includes over fifty articles for radical and Native newspapers and journals; poetry; short stories; the novels, *Sundogs* and *Ravensong: I Am Woman*, a collection of essays, stories and poetry; *Sojourner's Truth*, a short story collection; and *Bobbi Lee*, an autobiographical novel. She has four children and two grandchildren and presently lives near Toronto, Ontario.

JEANNETTE C. ARMSTRONG

Unclean Tides: An Essay on Salmon and Relations

The Pacific Coast is a lace work of streams, rivers and lakes flowing into the inlets, fjords and deltas along the ocean front of the mainland. The waters flow down from the mountains and plateaus to drain the interior spawning streams through rapid and icy cold rivers, on to the delta estuaries, in one of the richest salmon habitation sites of the world. Salmon have come home to these rivers for over an estimated one million years. All species of salmon—the Chinook which live longer, the red-fleshed sockeye, the coho, the silvery chum and the numerous small pinks—follow life cycles starting in the rivers, going out to the ocean and, finally, returning to the rivers to spawn.

For thousands of years the original peoples of the West Coast of North America practiced sustainable conservation harvesting through complex patterns of strictly observed trade laws and internal practice. In salmon harvesting, everyone observed ceremonially protected customs which imbedded respect for their source of life. Such customs, exampled by first salmon rites, are common throughout the Pacific North-west Coast peoples. Salmon harvesting was strictly regulated in various ways by knowledge-keeper chiefs in their various jurisdictions, no matter where on the river system, to allow for upstream takes with the goal of preserving future full spawning cycles. These conservation methods are the source of an original and inherent right of those peoples to continue to harvest and enjoy their ancestors' magnificent legacy.

Today all five salmon species are battling for their survival under the onslaught of the most severe pressures in their long history. In little over one century, the colonization of the Americas has laid to waste the results of thousands of years of good conservation practiced by original peoples.

In some areas, like the Okanagan Valley in British Columbia where I was raised, salmon have utterly disappeared, except for the several dozen miracle sockeye which somehow battle courageously over the many U.S. dams on the great Columbia and its tributaries to reach us. My relatives still celebrate the first salmon rites, though, as a child, I saw the last salmon harvests on the Okanagan River in our territory. We still pray for the return of the salmon, even while the loss to our people creates the deepest possible grief.

Where salmon is the most important source of life and the outward expression of God, the spirit of a whole people becomes wounded beyond expression when that source is annihilated. I have seen that deep despair in the many river peoples who can no longer harvest salmon. There are many such peoples in the U.S. and Canada who cannot practice their legal right to harvest for food or trade, though such rights were bitterly fought for and won in hostile courts. The salmon runs are gone, nearly extinct or so heavily polluted that eating them poses serious health risks.

In other areas, Native salmon food and trade harvesting in inland river fisheries is strictly restricted or prohibited by armed fishery officials, blaming the insignificant Native river fishing for the massive depletion of millions of salmon. Whether in Canada or the U.S., laws prioritize and protect spawning river salmon only to increase returns to the commercial ocean harvesters, who are allowed to intercept the biggest percentage of returning salmon before they reach the rivers. Meanwhile the strict regulations of the Native river fishing of U.S. Tribes and B.C. First Nations represent continued and willing strict observance to year-by-year conservation strategies. They observe the annually set counts for catches—first for ceremonial, then for food and last for trade.

Public and politically motivated government malice towards Native resistance of on-going, biased inequities and blatant scapegoating has generated explosive race-centered confrontations. This has provided governments with the justification to criminalize the very peoples whose conservation practices developed and preserved these salmon stocks—people who were never perpetrators of the self-centered, mindless "progress" instrumental in such destruction. People who, instead, should be thanked and held in the highest esteem and given first priority to harvest their regular catch. Native peoples, whose accumulated river catch numbered in the paltry thousands, harvest only a minute fraction of the huge millions harvested offshore. Native peoples continue to receive an extremely small percentage of commercial fishing, even with decisive court actions in the U.S.

and Canada reluctantly finding for equitable Native allocations.

The shameful history of the colonizing powers' hostilities and unwarranted aggressions toward Natives, in both Canada and the U.S., is eclipsed only by the appalling portrait of greed in the unrestricted and unregulated development throughout this century. It reveals the grim reality of ocean and river fishing and canning operations' over-harvesting and rapid destruction of whole salmon runs in the earlier half of the century. Even more ghastly is the entire picture of devastation inflicted by other heedless boom patterns coming out of the frontier mentality of the West. Habitat loss of spawning streams on both sides of the 49th parallel reached an acute level as a result of the cumulative and combined effects from widespread sources.

Urbanization and municipal planning, some of the major culprits along with road and rail construction, impeded and altered water levels and flow and created artificial watercourses and concrete canals. Industrial and urban wastes from huge city and rural populations filled lakes and rivers with a myriad of unpredictable contaminants, particles and excessive phosphates. Their excessive effluent encouraged the proliferation of alien plant forms and choked out important freshwater estuaries and lakes.

Agribusiness added increased salinity, farm sewage and carcinogenic pesticide drainage into major systems. In addition to these pollutants, the effects of flow controls, water displacements and huge stream diversions used for irrigation damaged spawning and estuary systems irreversibly.

Power dams blocked spawning migrations and killed fry and smolt in their turbines. Damming created huge alterations in river current, speed and depth, drastically changing water temperature, resulting in obliterated estuaries and non-viable or unattainable spawning areas.

Unregulated clear-cut logging operations caused erosion, which lead to silting and raging flood sedimentation suffocating salmon eggs and alevin. Milling and pulp operations added extensive wastes as well as deadly PCPs and other dioxins used in lumber preservation.

Mining pollution took its toll in unregulated heavy metal tailings flushed or leaked into lakes and rivers. Others released radioactive and toxic smelter by-products while massive hydraulic operations by placer mining destroyed highland stream spawning beds.

The introduction of foreign fish

183

Jeanette C. Armstrong

species into rivers, lakes and streams continues to create an untold risk and directly affects the survival rates of eggs, alevin, fry and smolt while also creating more competition for the same food sources.

❧

Salmon farming, once thought to be the answer to declining wild stocks, is now a major risk and competitor. While remaining a marginally viable option, the high incidence of disease in farmed fish results in low survival rates. Additionally, natural salmon stock genes are seriously threatened from interbreeding with farmed, genetically altered salmon. Wild salmon now face new bio-risks from mutated bacteria, parasites and fish viruses from salmon farm escapees, where genetically engineered salmon, enhanced by hormonal manipulations and transpecies gene splicing, rely on antibiotics to survive. Most disturbing is a general decline in size and weight of all five wild Pacific salmon species and the disappearance of whole spawning runs.

The states of Washington and Oregon have compromised their salmon rivers and tributaries to the extent of allowing the most profound depletions and extinctions. American West Coast commercial fisheries are virtually dead. Once thriving coastal fishing communities from California to Washington have become ghost towns. The worst symptom, perhaps, is revealed in the disputes over the dying fisheries illustrated by the open warfare between sport fishers, environmentalists and legal Tribal harvesters over the few remaining runs in places where rivers are blocked by the most numerous dams in the world. These are places where rivers, now faced with total extinctions of salmon stocks, once produced salmon in the millions; places where salmon stocks are endangered beyond rescue from radiation leaks and other deep level contaminations; places where even the American Pacific commercial fleets (except Alaska), having committed their own suicidal demise, have disappeared like the canneries in *Cannery Row*.

While British Columbia has not dammed its rivers to such a great extent and has thus preserved healthier runs, its salmon fisheries are quickly moving toward the same consequence as the American fisheries. Declines in the British Columbian fisheries have become serious due to a wide variety of other destructive sources.

Forestry, the leading industry in British Columbia, is taking its toll on the rivers and spawning systems. The

Fishing in Lillooet on the Fraser River. Jackie Kruger holds the net while Brian Tom looks at the catch.

Department of Fisheries and Oceans (DFO) announced a series of amendments in January, 1997, including a three-year, fifteen-million-dollar habitat enhancement and salmon restoration program. Stringent legislation in the new Forestry Practice Act has slowly begun implementing codes for stream and waterway protection. Forest Renewal, legislated as a formal government program in B.C., has begun long overdue projects for reversal of the devastating effects of past poor logging practices.

Logging operations and clear-cuts have not been the only culprits. Industrial pollution from various operations has contributed a lion's share of contamination. The largest cities and farming communities in B.C. are built on river delta systems and its major inland watercourses through which the salmon must pass to spawn in smaller streams and creeks. A prime example is the lower Fraser, Canada's third largest urban area and home to almost two million people. Over one-third of the streams in the Lower-Fraser Basin are now devoid of salmon.

The Fisheries Act, one of the most progressive of environmental legislations in the world, still fails to defend against the destruction of salmon-bearing streams by urban spread. The provincial government has been equally ineffective in its development guidelines which were coupled with the federal-provincial habitat protection initiatives for stream stewardship. A whole-system rethinking of growth and urban sprawl is required to have healthy streams, according to Otto Langer, chair of DFO's Habitat Council. So while a current view in Canada is that stream stewardship in urban areas must be linked to seemingly unrelated issues to be effective (like municipal zoning), this requires cumbersome multilevel government agreements.

There is no doubt Canada's Pacific salmon fisheries are in acute crisis and the problem is a complex one of internal and external forces. Although still productive, the salmon industry in Canada is now reacting to the effects of overall

Jeanette C. Armstrong

Jeannette Armstrong's mother, Lilly, shows Jeannette, age 14, and friend, Marlene Squakin, how to slice thin fillets so the fish will dry quickly.

declines. In March 1996, Canada's Federal Department of Fisheries and Oceans Minister, Fred Mifflin, passed legislation seeking to reduce commercial salmon fleets by buying back 800 licenses from commercial salmon fishers. Licenses were given for fixed areas along the coast. The result was that fishers who wish to pursue access to more than one region must buy out licenses from other fishers. This served to decrease boat numbers in the fleet, but stimulated big investment buy-outs.

Fleets of independent and small-boat fishers have disappeared. Small fishing communities which once thrived on trolling and other forms of small-boat fishing and processing are now emptying, wiping out whole cultures, Native and non-Native, creating unemployment and comprehensively destroying a more locally sustainable way of life. Yet vanishing salmon runs are blamed on inland river Native food and trade fishing by the remaining competing interests.

Ninety percent of the salmon caught in British Columbia is allocated to the commercial fleet, while the other ten percent is shared by sports and tribal fisheries. In the past, big-boat seine fleets accounted for over half the commercial catch. Under the Mifflin Plan, the commercial fleet squeezed out small-boat gill-netters and trollers from coastal communities, leaving a big company, urban-based industry. It did nothing to reduce the commercial salmon catch. All that took place was to enhance big-business seining and replace local community economies with transnational corporate control.

❧

The Fraser River is the largest source of sockeye salmon in the world, supporting 100 distinct stocks. Sockeye account for fifty percent of the total salmon catch in the Fraser River. Sockeye had increased from approximately five million in the early 1980s to over fifteen million on its dominant cycles in the second half of the 1990s, due to Canada's spending on increasing spawning escapement targets. In 1990 the total annual run of sockeye salmon in all of British Columbia was fourteen million, but at the beginning of this century the Fraser River salmon run alone was over thirty million.

Ten million sockeye are taken from the Fraser stocks each year with eighteen percent of the Fraser run taken by

U.S. commercial fishing in the Strait of Juan de Fuca and, to a lesser extent, in Southeast Alaska. The U.S. net fisheries in Washington State waters are now directing increasing efforts at the Fraser River sockeye. The Johnston Strait accounts for the majority of Canadian catch followed by a smaller catch in the Strait of Juan de Fuca and the Strait of Georgia and off the West Coast of Vancouver Island and B.C.'s North Coast.

The Nass and Skeena River sockeye runs, though smaller, have historically continued a steady production of over four million sockeye. However, the sockeye from these rivers mature on the high seas in the Gulf of Alaska and return to the Nass and Skeena, passing through Southeast Alaskan fisheries where large numbers are now being intercepted.

Over sixty percent of sockeye taken in Southeast Alaska are Canadian-origin sockeye. Alaskan interceptions of Canadian stocks from these two rivers have more than doubled since the signing of the Pacific Salmon Treaty in 1985, with catches now totaling over one million a year. The Noyes Island and Tree Point commercial U.S. fisheries take twenty-five percent of the Skeena River catch and fifty percent of the Nass River catch, in some years making it

Jeanette C. Armstrong

impossible for Canada to meet its minimum escapement goals for conservation of those stocks for spawning returns. As a consequence these stocks are now threatened with rapid declines.

In comparison, in the river stock management and conservation between British Columbia and Southeast Alaska, joint enhancement projects of sockeye from the transboundary rivers have increased returns to both Canadian and Alaskan fisheries. The 1995 Yukon Salmon Agreement, mandated under the Treaty and reached after similar agreements on the Yukon River stocks, promises similar success.

The Chinook salmon rebuilding program initiated under the Pacific Salmon Treaty was to reduce fishing of the severely threatened Chinook by fifty percent to encourage escapement. But Chinook migration along the coasts of Oregon, Washington, British Columbia and Alaska occurred through a sequence of historically unrestricted commercial fisheries, leading to severe over-harvesting of stocks before the signing of the treaty. The U.S. and Canada agreed to reduce Chinook harvests as a conservation program to rebuild stocks at mutually agreed upon levels for the major Chinook fisheries in Canada and Alaska.

Although an initial small increase was achieved, rebuilding Chinook stocks has slowed on the West Coast of Vancouver Island as a result of recent unfavorable ocean conditions. Prior levels of harvesting reduction are now insufficient to ensure the rebuilding of depleted stocks, due to higher than normal water temperatures and predation of young salmon by mackerel. Over fifty percent of the Chinook stocks under conservation are not rebuilding, with West Coast Vancouver Island stocks now in a critical state.

Although the rebuilding program directly benefits the U.S. Chinook stocks originating in Washington and Oregon, Alaskan authorities have been unwilling to cooperate (or operate) in Chinook conservation actions and unwilling to agree to lower reduction levels required by recent ocean conditions. A U.S. civil law suit provided the only stop-gap in ordering an early closure to American commercial Chinook takes in 1996 and 1997. While Canada has achieved its fifty percent target reductions for the West Coast of Vancouver Island and the North Coast of B.C., thereby reducing Canadian impact on U.S. stocks in accordance with the rebuilding program, the Alaskan fisheries harvest rates continue at pre-1994 levels.

In comparison, the lower Georgia Strait Canadian Chinook fishery is predicted to reach rebuilding goals in 1998.

It has been rapidly rebuilding since 1988 when Canada introduced severely restrictive fishery measures in all harvesting including First Nations and sports harvesting.

The coho conservation program reduced limits to Canadian commercial trolling off the West Coast of Vancouver Island and closed the commercial net fishery at the southern end of Vancouver Island. Since 1985, this coho fishery has been the only coho fishery subjected to a catch limit under the treaty. This has directly benefited U.S. coho stocks by reducing interceptions of U.S.-origin coho. However poor ocean survival conditions and deteriorating habitat are resulting in declines of these stocks.

The recent Georgia Strait migrations of southern B.C. coho stocks to the West Coast of Vancouver Island has created grave concerns for conservation. Canada reduced its harvest rate by further stringent restrictions on the Strait of Georgia troll and sport fisheries.

In northern B.C., concerns mount as problems worsen for coho stocks. Severe over-fishing has escalated through interceptions by fisheries in Southeast Alaska, where there are no agreed limits to protect Canadian-origin coho. Between 1984 and 1995 Alaskan coho interceptions increased from 350,000 to 1.4 million. Conservation of the Skeena River coho has reached an acute level where returns reached record lows in 1992 and 1993, predicting the current plummeting declines.

Southeast Alaska takes sixty-five percent of the ocean coho catch. Since 1990 the U.S. troll fisheries on Canadian stocks doubled. In comparison, Canada has closed coho fisheries entirely and severely restricted others by up to fifty percent reductions on these northern fisheries.

One result of the continued abuses and corruptions involved in the big-business over-fishing of depleted American salmon stocks has resulted in an American big-business fishing sentiment of power and privilege. This sentiment, historically directed toward Native legal

The Okanagan way of spiraling strips of salmon around the drying sticks. In the background is a pan of bread cooking over the fire.

Jeanette C. Armstrong

fishing and sports fishing, has shifted to government environmental regulation and open aggressions toward healthier Canadian salmon stocks which can be intercepted in American waters. The impacts of over-harvesting by U.S. commercial fishing, combined with non-compliance of an agreed-to joint responsibility, now creates a serious domestic dilemma among Canada's Pacific salmon fishing industry, conservation programs and international trade relations with the United States. Canada's apparent loss of sovereign control over its fishing industry can be seen as a symptom of a much deeper looming global problem of big-business corporate interests securing international priorities over domestic local economies and environmental concerns.

The signing of the Pacific Salmon Treaty in 1985 between Canada and the U.S. established two basic principles of a shared responsibility for conservation and equity. Despite the agreement, blatant disregard for "responsible" actions has occurred. The principles obliged the two parties to prevent over-fishing and provide for optimum production, while ensuring each country receive fishery benefits equivalent to the production of salmon from its own rivers, thereby balancing interceptions and promoting direct consequence for conservation

measures. Current statistics document U.S. interceptions on Canadian-origin salmon have increased by fifty percent while Canadian interceptions of U.S.-origin salmon decreased by twenty-five percent.

Pacific Salmon Treaty talks began again in 1992, when the original treaty expired. Talks centered on the concerns over the increasing interceptions of endangered Chinook by U.S. fishers and interceptions of endangered U.S. coho by Canadian fishers. The U.S. refused to negotiate in a serious way resulting in Canada's imposed transit fees on U.S. fishermen. Despite direct intervention in 1994 by U.S. Vice President Al Gore, talks continued to fail. A third party, jointly paid-for mediator was needed. The secret mediation report prepared by New Zealand Ambassador Christopher Beeby, a World Trade Judge, was rejected by the U.S., according to Canadian officials. Leaked reports cited the document to have sided with Canada's claim of American over-fishing and suggested American curtailment or compensation. An attempt at mediation in 1996 broke down and Canada asked for binding arbitration. The U.S. refused.

Hostilities between the two countries have since erupted even more seriously, with political pressure coming loudly from state and provincial business agendas. In 1997, talks broke down after Canada's seizure of four U.S. fishing vessels in Canadian waters followed by B.C.'s threats to close a U.S. torpedo testing range on Vancouver Island. The U.S. southern Alaskan commercial fishers retaliated by hauling in an unprecedented five times their regular Canadian salmon interceptions. This inordinately ignorant and dangerous move has struck fear in the B.C. Native food and trade fishers monitoring the ominously low river returns. Under their own severely restrictive conservation programs, it has forced them to voluntarily cut their 1997 river and ocean fishing to almost nothing—again. For most First Nations who depend on the salmon runs it means no income and, in some communities, a seriously inadequate food supply.

The end consequence will be a tragic and more rapid decline of the West Coast of North America's salmon populations. Like the buffalo herds of the Great Plains and the cod off the East Coast of North America, the Pacific Salmon are moving toward disappearance in an increasing tide of malevolence. The salmon are, ironically, more threatened by economic and political forces. Forces which are well-informed on environmental consequence and should therefore more easily be brought

to order than the earlier unruly burgeoning of frontier building. Corporate economic interests and a subservient government political agenda continue this kind of outrageous irresponsibility in outright abandonment of principles in the face of widespread and informed opposition. There are growing numbers of aware and conscientious citizens in Canada and the U.S. who are beginning to see that the dissolving national boundaries on today's international trade economics require detached, big-business aggression over small business, because strong local economies stimulate local responsibility and therefore better controls.

Rather than to fall into the easy trap of patriotism, the most illuminating approach to the 1997 salmon war tactics might be to look at why *not* having an agreement in place for as long as possible best suits big-business stakeholders who sit at the negotiating table. It may be worthwhile to focus on the thousands of small-boat fishers and fish traders, Native and non-Native, now unemployed on both sides of the border, and their rights. It may be important to pay heed to the rights of the sixty thousand B.C. school children and eight thousand parent groups, and others like them in the U.S., rebuilding salmon spawning beds with their hands and to ask who

Jeanette C. Armstrong

should be the beneficiary of such work. It may be critical to ally these with conservationist academics and Native groups in both countries, in an exercise of real democracy for the people, and move against government pandering to big business and reclaim the smaller local economies, insuring the basic ingredient of responsible sustainable practice.

It is no longer a simple matter of voting for the right amendments, bills or parties in each of our respective corners. The loyalties of sane people can no longer blindly be for the misguided systems which move us all into oblivion. Rather, we must forge something new, a new course chosen for the right reasons. A course insuring the preservation of the precious gifts of life to each of us and our generations to come as true caretakers of these lands. For the salmon—our spirit relatives, messengers of the future —are swimming the unclean tides heralding our passing, and in their ebb speak of the duty entrusted to each of us born in this time of grave omens.

References:

American Friends Service Committee. *Uncommon Controversy: Fishing Rights of the Muckleshoot, Puyallup and Nisqually Indians.* Seattle: University of Washington Press, 1970.

Aquatic News Network. "First Nations, Other Groups Unite on Fish Farm Concerns." Press Release. 21 January 1997.

Beudry, Michael. "Searching for Sockeye." *Equinox,* December 1992.

British Columbia Hydro and Power Authority. *Air Land Water Managing Resources Responsibly.* B.C. Hydro Report on the Environment. Victoria, 1997.

British Columbia. Ministry of Environment. "Salmon Enhancement Program Annual Report Summary." *British Columbia Government Supply and Services.* Victoria, 1992.

British Columbia. Provincial Archives. Provincial Museum. *Interior Salish.* Ser. 1, "British Columbia Heritage Series"; vol. 3, "Our Native Peoples." 1952.

British Columbia Provincial Government. Office of the Premier. "B.C. Ends Seabed Lease for Nanoose Torpedo Range in Response to US Intransigence on Salmon Talks." Press Release. 23 May 1997.

Canada. Department of Fisheries and Oceans. *Pacific Region Vision 2000.* Discussion Draft. Ottawa, 1989.

Canada. Department of Foreign Affairs and International Trade. Department of Fisheries and Oceans. *The Pacific Salmon Treaty: An Overview.* Ottawa, 1996.

Canada. Environment Canada. "A State of the Environment Report: Pollutants in British Columbia's Marine Environment." *Supply and Services Canada.* SOE Report, no. 89-1. Ottawa, 1989.

Canada. Provincial Government. B.C. Aboriginal Peoples' Fisheries Commission. *Towards Mutual Purpose And Support.* Pre-Season Assembly Report. Victoria, 1990.

Colville Confederated Tribes. Fish and Wildlife Department. *Colville Indian Reservation Tribal Member Fishing Regulations.* Resolution 1996-174. Nespelem, WA, 1996.

Drucker, Philip. *Cultures of the North Pacific Coast.* Vancouver, B.C.: Chandler Publishing, 1965.

Glavin, Terry. "Coho in the Culverts." *Canadian Geographic.* May/June 1997.

Hollowell, Christopher. "Farmers of the Sea." *Time Magazine.* 28 October 1996.

Howard, Ross and Craig McInnes. "B.C. Declares Salmon War: Clark Wants Ottawa to Assemble Armada in Retaliation for Alaskan Catch." *Globe and Mail.* 18 July 1997.

Hume, Mark. *The Run of the River: Portraits of Eleven British Columbia Rivers.* Vancouver, B.C.: New Star Books, 1992.

Hunter, Justine. "Report on Salmon War Backs Canada." *Vancouver Sun.* 17 May 1997.

Legal Services Society of British Columbia. Native Programs Department. *Fishing—Aboriginal Rights in British Columbia.* Annual Report. Victoria, 1995.

Opinion/Editorials. "Yet Another Collapse in U.S. Canada Fish Talks." *The Seattle Times.* 25 May 1997.

Stewart, Hilary. *Indian Fishing: Early Methods on the Northwest Coast.* Seattle: University of Washington Press, 1977.

"The Comprehensive Research Report on Native Affairs and Issues." *Native Issues Monthly.* December 1994–November 1997.

U.S. Department of the Interior. *Indian Fishing Rights in the Pacific Northwest.* A special report prepared by the Office of the Special Assistant to the Secretary of the Interior Pacific Northwest Region. Portland, OR, 1974.

Ware, Reuben M. "Five Issues Five Battlegrounds." In *An Introduction to the History of Indian Fishing in British Columbia 1850–1930.* Chiliwack, B.C.: Coqualeetza Education Training Centre, 1983.

193

Jeanette C. Armstrong

JEANNETTE C. ARMSTRONG (Okanagan) lives on the Penticton Indian Reservation. A fluent speaker of the Okanagan language, she has studied under some of the most knowledgeable Elders of the Okanagan. She holds a degree in fine arts from the University of Victoria. Her visual works have been recognized through awards and she is an established Canadian author. Her published works include two award-winning children's books, the critically acclaimed novel *Slash*, a collection of poetry, *Breath Tracks*, and a collaboration with Native architect Douglas Cardinal, *Native Creative Process*. She has been anthologized frequently and has published poetry and articles in a wide variety of journals. Her other creative works include two produced video scripts and productions of poetry/music collaborations, *Indian Woman* and *Till the Bars Break*, as well as local and national TV appearances and performances.

Jeannette is also the director of the En'owkin International School of Writing, a university-accredited Native school and has been an active advocate for Native rights. She has addressed conferences and assemblies on a wide range of topics in Japan, Moscow, Switzerland, German and New Zealand as well as in the U.S. and Canada.

SHIGERU KAYANO

The Fox's Plea: An Ainu Fable

Translated by
Jane Corddry Langill
with Rie Taki

This fable belongs to the genre of uepeker, *prose folktales told around the fire pit by Ainu elders, who often included a moral lesson at the end. This is the title story of* Kitsune no Charanke, *a collection of tales that were recorded from recitations in Ainu, and then translated into Japanese and compiled into a book for children by Shigeru Kayano. Mr. Kayano spent many evenings in his childhood sitting by the hearth, listening to his grandmother tell stories much like this one.*

The title of the story refers to a special type of oral argument, the charanke. *In addition to the vast literature of ancient epic poetry, which was memorized and handed down by skilled chanters, the Ainu were said to be great storytellers and speakers in everyday life, where fluency in argument was a prized skill and disputes were often settled with a war of words instead of swords. In this story, it is the spirit of a fox who employs the human technique of the* charanke *to plead for the non-human creatures who share the natural world. Throughout the fable, the word Ainu means "human being."*

Up near Lake Shikotsu, in a place called Usakumai, there lived a young Ainu of very good heart. His village was nestled next to high mountains full of deer and bear, so whenever he was hungry, he would take up his bow and arrow and head out into the hills. He always caught plenty of deer and bear, which he brought back to share with the neighbors or make into smoked meat. He enjoyed a happy and peaceful life with his family.

Nearby, there flowed a river with beautiful clear water, and in the autumn many salmon swam up the river to spawn. Ainu came from all around, even from as far away as the village of Biratori, to catch those salmon and preserve them for their winter food stores.

Of course, Ainu were not the only ones who depended on the salmon for food. The other animals who lived up in the mountains also survived by catching the fish when they swam upstream. All the creatures lived happily and peacefully together, sharing the salmon without disturbing one another.

The Chitose River starts at Lake Shikotsu, runs through the city of Chitose, flows into the giant Ishikari River and travels hundreds of miles across Hokkaido and into the Sea of Japan.

The years of such a peaceful life went swiftly by and the young Ainu grew old. After awhile, he no longer went up into the mountains to hunt for bear but stayed at home and worked at making beautiful carvings of wood.

One night he worked late, as was his habit, then crawled into bed. He was just dozing off when he heard a human voice, far in the distance. Wondering who would be coming at such a late hour, he strained his ears to listen, but the voice disappeared. When he laid his head back down on the pillow, the voice sounded again.

Thinking it strange, he quietly pulled off his quilt and crept out of the house, taking care not to wake his family. Outside, the moon was shining brightly, so if he looked very hard, he could see far into the distance.

He faced towards the sound of the voice and began to walk slowly in that direction, keeping his footfall as quiet as possible. As he drew closer, the voice sounded less and less like that of a human being. It seemed to be coming from across the river, from the opposite bank.

So he continued on quietly. When he focused his gaze on the place where the voice came from, he saw Fox sitting there. Fox was speaking rapidly and earnestly about something, using the language of humans. Listening more carefully, the Ainu realized that Fox was delivering a *charanke* (an impassioned plea) and that it was directed at human beings.

"All you Ainu, listen well! Ainu did not create the salmon, nor did we Foxes. The spirits who reign at the mouth of the Ishikari River, the god Pipirinoekur and the goddess Pipirinoemat, want to ensure that all the creatures who eat salmon will have enough to share. Every year, when the salmon come home to spawn, these gods decide how many fish will come up this river. Indeed, they send enough fish so that even after you Ainu, we Foxes, Bear and all the other salmon-eating creatures have had our fill, there will still be some left over.

"But today, when I helped myself to just one of many salmon that an Ainu had caught and left on the bank, that Ainu cursed me with a whole array of insults. His ugly words enveloped me, like black flames. Not only that, but that Ainu also made an appeal to all the Gods to banish Foxes from living in the same land as Ainu! I fear that the Gods may listen to that Ainu and send the Foxes to some distant, barren mountain, some wretched place without grass or trees where even Birds could not survive. This situation is unbearable. I appeal to all the Gods and all the Ainu to listen to our plea!"

This is what Fox said, speaking with great sadness as tears welled up in his eyes. As he spoke, he held his pointed ears up straight and swished his tail from side to side.

The virtuous old Ainu was shocked to hear this. Everything that Fox had said was right and proper.

The Ainu are not the only ones with the right to eat fish. The Gods give the gift of fish for food to all creatures who need them to survive. One foolish Ainu who did not remember this had gravely insulted the God of the Foxes. (You see, when an animal or plant needs to deliver a *charanke*, it becomes a God and can speak in the language of Ainu.)

The next morning, the wise old Ainu called together all the people of the village. He thoroughly reprimanded the foolish Ainu who had insulted the Fox God and ordered him to offer his precious sword as restitution. They brewed rice wine and carved special offerings of shaved willow wood, and they presented these to the God of the Foxes with their profound apologies.

Witnessing all of this, the other Gods decided not to banish the Foxes to a distant land, but rather to allow them to live forever in the land of the Ainu.

"So remember, all of you Ainu who hear this. The fish in the rivers and fruit on the trees are made for all creatures to share. We must never imagine that these are intended for Ainu only."

With these final words, the virtuous Ainu departed this world.

(*Translated from Japanese.*)

199

Shigeru Kayano